RACING
THROUGH THE NIGHT
OLYMPIC'S ATTEMPT
TO REACH *TITANIC*

WADE SISSON

AMBERLEY

For Mom and Dad,
the anchors of our family; to Cade, Maggie, Aaron and Carey,
with compasses true; and to Avery, Reegan, Marrit, Roslyn and Corben,
the wind in our sails.

First published 2011

Amberley Publishing
The Hill, Stroud
Gloucestershire, GL5 4EP

www.amberley-books.com

British Library Cataloguing in Publication Data.
A catalogue record for this book is available from the British Library.

ISBN 978 1 4456 0026 0

Typeset in 10pt on 12pt Sabon.
Typesetting and Origination by Amberley Publishing.
Printed in the UK.

Hull – Selby

York – Scarborough

Weaverthorpe Station.

York – Scarborough

Cayton Station.

Contents

Captain Edward J. Smith took many of the crew of *Adriatic* onto *Olympic* and, subsequently, *Titanic*. The surgeon, purser and chief steward of *Adriatic* would all die on *Titanic* with Captain Smith. (J & C McCutcheon Collection)

Olympic opened for public inspection on May 27 1911. She would sail for Liverpool and Southampton on 31 May, soon after *Titanic*'s launch. (J & C McCutcheon Collection)

Introduction

This book was born of my desire to read the incredible tale you're about to enjoy. In all my years as a *Titanic* buff, I've always wondered what it was like to be on the *Titanic*'s nearly identical sister ship, *Olympic*, on the night disaster struck.

Pieces of the story are spread throughout the voluminous writings from 1912 to the present day – from old newspaper clippings and interviews to the hundreds of books and stories that have followed. But they were always just that – pieces. Tantalizing, fascinating – but never gathered in one place to form a complete narrative.

This book is my attempt to collect, form and share that narrative.

What was it like to be on the *Olympic* that night? What were the passengers told? How did they feel when they learned their ship's twin had sunk?

So, that became the mission of this book – to tell that story in as complete a manner as possible. The very name *Titanic* has become so well-known in our world that it is easy to forget that she was one of three sister ships – and that the eldest sister was the one that got most of the attention and acclaim. Until April 14, 1912, that is.

This is the story of the RMS *Olympic*, her role in the *Titanic* story and the lessons – both learned and unlearned – that contributed to the famous disaster.

As Walter Lord wrote at the conclusion to *A Night to Remember*, 'It is a rash man indeed who would set himself up as final arbiter on all that happened the incredible night the *Titanic* went down.'

I couldn't agree more. Even now, nearly 100 years on, we continue to learn more about the *Titanic* and her sisters every day. May this story add to the great narrative, and may new information continue to come to light.

Wade Sisson
January 2011

About the Author

Wade's fascination with the *Titanic* began when he was in the sixth grade. While working on a book report assignment, he came upon a book with a drawing of a big ship on the cover. The ship was heading right for an iceberg. The book was *A Night to Remember* – and the ship was, of course, the *Titanic*.

Like many *Titanic* buffs, Wade was drawn in by Walter Lord's wonderful ability to 'take us there.' Lord made that night come alive – and for people around the world, the story of the *Titanic* remains as vivid today as it was on that night back in 1912.

A few years later, Wade learned that there was an organization of people who shared his interest, and he joined the Titanic Historical Society. That same year, the wreck of the *Titanic* was discovered, and suddenly *Titanic* was in the news again. The apogee came in 1997 with James Cameron's epic film *Titanic*, and suddenly *Titanic* was everywhere.

Wade always dreamed of writing a book about the *Titanic*, but he wasn't sure he'd ever find an aspect of the disaster that hadn't already been covered time and time again. Then he remembered something that had always fascinated him: *Titanic*'s sister ship, *Olympic*. She was always a footnote to the story of April 14–15, 1912 – until now.

CHAPTER 1
'Message Received; It's SOS'

Just a day and a half out of New York on her twentieth transatlantic crossing, the luxury liner *Olympic* steamed across the surface of a glassy sea on an easterly course toward England. On this moonless Sunday night, April 14, 1912, the ship's hull was illuminated from stem to stern by row upon row of portholes that cut through the darkness, rivaled only by the vast expanse of stars overhead.

To the nearly 2,000 people on board, she was the last word in comfort – a floating palace designed to cater to their every whim. But on this trip, for the first time since her maiden voyage the previous June, *Olympic* was experiencing something of a demotion.

For nearly a year *Olympic* had enjoyed her status as the biggest ocean liner in the world and all the pomp and publicity the title brought. But the previous Wednesday, as *Olympic* eased into her New York pier, the 882-foot ship had enjoyed for the last time the title, 'Biggest steamer in the world.'

As *The New York Times* reported, 'As the *Olympic* steamed into New York harbor, her sister ship the *Titanic* started on her maiden voyage from Southampton for this city. Therefore the *Olympic* has made her last trip to New York as the biggest ship afloat. Hereafter she will share that honor with her 45,000 ton sister ship the *Titanic*.'[1]

In fact, the honor was already being shared. Just a few hours before *Olympic*'s arrival in New York on Wednesday, April 10, the *Titanic* had departed Southampton, England.

Even now, as *Olympic* cut her path eastward, *Titanic* was in mid-Atlantic, only a few days from her first arrival in America.

New York was accustomed to harboring the world's great steamships and bearing witness to their arrivals and departures. In recent years the port had seen the size of ships grow to unprecedented size – so large, in fact, that her piers had to be extended in order to accommodate the latest, greatest steamships.

Now the city's press was doing double-duty, noting the *Olympic*'s departure and alerting the public to *Titanic*'s imminent arrival. As *The New York Times* reported on April 14:[2]

SAILING OF *OLYMPIC* STARTS RUSH ABROAD

Giant White Star Liner Off with a Notable List of Passengers.

GREAT THRONG AT THE PIER

With a list of passengers indicating that the Summer rush to Europe is beginning, the White Star liner *Olympic* got off for Southampton at 3 o'clock yesterday afternoon. A large crowd was at the pier to watch the second biggest ship in the world sail – the *Titanic* now being the largest – and despite the fact that a cold wind was blowing through the pier the scene looked like one of the late Spring sailings when the rush to the other side is in full swing.

Like her sister ship, *Olympic*'s passenger list was filled with notables from all corners of American and European society.

Among her first class passengers were Lord and Lady Ashburton. Lord Ashburton, a renowned English sportsman, had enjoyed a trip to the Rockies to hunt big game. Such was his delight with the hunt that he announced his intention to return again next year.

Lady Ashburton, the former Frances Belmont of New York, had just been featured in an American newspaper as one of three 'American chorus girls [to] have married titled Englishmen, and so far their marriages have been very happy.'[3] Lady Ashburton had come to New York bearing a special present for each of her three American sisters – coats and muffs made from the furs of 5,000 moles trapped on her English estate.[4]

Claude Casimir-Perier, son of the late President of France, was returning to Europe with his wife following a long visit to America that had begun the previous fall. The Casimir-Periers were a very prominent family in France. Indeed, young Claude's ancestry included a father, grandfather and great-grandfather who were all in turn prime ministers.

During his American tour, Casimir-Perier made notes for a report he would later issue to the French government recommending improvements to French ports and railway systems. His travels took him through Boston, New York, Philadelphia and Baltimore, Mobile, Alabama, and New Orleans. From there he travelled to Texarkana, Los Angeles, San Diego, San Francisco, Portland and Vancouver. From there he returned direct by train to New York City in time to board *Olympic*.[5]

On sailing day, Casimir-Perier shared his overall thoughts in a wireless message issued to his country and reported in *The New York Times*. Declaring that 'Trouble is ahead for America,' Casimir-Perier shared his opinion that the United States was 'committing one of the worst mistakes in her commercial history by the way in which she now is scattering harbors indiscriminately up and down both coasts.'[6]

Mrs Casimir-Perier, who was better known as the French actress of the stage name Madame Simone, had divorced her actor husband but was not able to marry Casimir-Perier as soon as she had hoped. The would-be groom's father objected to the marriage on the ground that Mme Simone was divorced. Mme Simone promised to postpone marriage for five years and kept her word. During the long engagement period, Claude's father died.[7]

The Casimir-Perier marriage in November 1909 scandalized the upper echelons of French society, much as the marriage of John Jacob Astor to Madeleine Force would scandalize New York society two years later, but the match did find some popular support.

The Mayor of Paris toasted the young couple. Of the bride he said, 'You, Madame, are famous as an actress. Your appearance upon one of our Parisian stages at an age when debuts, as a rule, yield only promises for the future, was a revelation. You have essentially a personal and original talent: an ardent, passionate, and sincere nature. You impersonate with singularly intense and living expression the heroines of that modern stage which is, perhaps, a trifle brutal, but which is endowed with undeniable dramatic force, and which pleases because it interests and moves the public.'

Mrs Casimir-Perier had joined her husband on his travels in the United States and, as she would later recall, was surprised by what she found there. 'I really couldn't have believed that I should have so much enjoyed living among Americans. I imagined them very different from what they are, and I made the mistake of thinking them more like the French. I found them extremely sympathetic and eager to be amused or instructed.'[8]

American banker Mortimer Schiff and his family were travelling to Europe for an extended vacation. The only son of German-Jewish banker and philanthropist Jacob Schiff, Mortimer was a partner in the financial firm Kuhn, Loeb & Co. but was perhaps best known for his efforts to establish the Boy Scouts of America.

The Schiffs had just won a reprieve in an on-going legal drama. On March 28 a grand jury found that neither Mortimer Schiff nor his attorney were guilty of conspiracy in causing Schiff's former valet to be sent to prison for thirty years for alleged burglary in the Schiff home. While the legal wrangling would continue, for now they had a resolution, and the former valet, Foulke E. Brandt, was free on bail.[9]

Tonight had been cause for celebration for one couple in first class. The Honorable Cyril Augustus Ward, a 36-year old British nobleman who had achieved the rank of Captain in the Royal Navy, was celebrating the eighth anniversary of his marriage to Baroness Irene de Brienen, a Dutch heiress.[10]

Revd Robert Hugh Benson was returning to England following the conclusion of his lecture series in the United States. Benson had created quite a stir in 1903 when he left the priesthood of the Church of England for which his late father, Edward White Benson, Archbishop of Canterbury, had been the spiritual head, in order to become a Catholic priest.

With his religious conversion, and his poems and novels on the subject of faith, Benson's adventures occasionally took him down some rather unorthodox paths.

A few days before his departure on *Olympic*, he spent the night in a Brooklyn house that was said to be haunted in order to 'seek the ghost' in company with a British journalist and another priest.[11]

Famed conductor Arturo Toscanini of the Metropolitan Opera House was travelling to Europe, where he intended to spend a short time in his native Italy before moving on to conduct the performances at the Buenos Aires Opera House in the summer.[12]

English painter Sir Alfred East was also on board ship for this crossing. The artist, whose paintings created a sensation wherever they toured, had been awarded a knighthood by King Edward VII, whose reign had defined the kind of leisurely, luxury-filled living that would become known as the Edwardian era. *Olympic* catered to this life perfectly.

On the second night out, *Olympic's* passengers were still finding their bearings on the immense ship. First class passengers were accustomed to luxury, and on *Olympic* there was plenty of it to be found.

The ship boasted a squash racquet court and gymnasium. She was only the second steamer in history to offer her passengers a swimming pool. Cabins and suites were decorated in a variety of period styles, complete with heavy reproduction furniture, fireplaces and electric lights and heaters.

The vast promenade decks stretched along most of the ship's length, and the ship's band provided lively music through every meal, as they had tonight. Live music in 1912 was a welcome novelty that provided immense enjoyment for passengers on ships of the day.

The first formal dress dinner had been served earlier that evening in the immense First Class Dining Saloon, which White Star Line publicity noted was the largest room afloat. Running the full 92-foot width of the ship, the vast room could accommodate 550 passengers at a single sitting.

Regardless of class, it was common practice for shipboard activity to be concluded early on Sundays, and by midnight most of the ship's company had retired to the warmth and comfort of their cabins.

Far removed from the luxury of First Class, *Olympic's* senior wireless operator Ernie Moore was still at work in the small wireless cabin, situated on the ship's highest deck – the Boat Deck – 40 feet behind the ship's bridge at the after end of the officer's quarters. The room was sparse save for the mass of wires and equipment that comprised the Marconi apparatus.[13]

Olympic's wireless operators rarely left their isolated cabin – with no porthole to enjoy the view – as the two took shifts in order to provide 24-hour wireless service. Their one luxury was a skylight in their cabin's ceiling that provided sunshine during the day and moonlight by night.

Together Moore and the junior operator, Alec Bagot, transmitted and received wireless messages that flowed in ceaselessly in an odd mix that included company business for the White Star Line, navigational information from other ships and personal messages for and from *Olympic's* passengers.

Olympic and *Titanic* were fitted with the most powerful Marconi wireless telegraphs then in use on the North Atlantic, giving each ship a minimum receiving and transmitting range of more than 250 miles.

Moore was just ending another long shift as his relief, Bagot, slept in the operators' bunk one door away. With the ship's proximity to shore, Moore was monitoring ship-to-shore chatter from the wireless station at Cape Race, Newfoundland. Tonight's news wasn't terribly exciting. In fact, he noted it was a repetition of the news he'd been getting since the ship left New York yesterday afternoon.

At about 12:40 a.m., Moore turned his powerful Marconi set from Cape Race traffic back to the commercial wavelength to tune in to any ship-to-ship messages then being sent.

He heard a ship with call sign MGY calling other ships and took note. MGY, he knew, was the call sign for *Olympic's* new sister ship, *Titanic. Titanic* was signaling about some ship that had struck an iceberg.

The signal wasn't as strong as it should be – too much atmospheric interference – and a number of other ships were signaling at the same time, jamming the signal further.

Moore was confused. Was it *Titanic* that was calling for help or some other ship? He broke into the chatter to ask if *Titanic* needed help.

A full 10 minutes passed before *Titanic* sent her reply: 'I require immediate assistance. Position 41.46 N, 50.14 W.'

Moore replied briskly 'RD. O.K,' which stood for 'Message Received. Understood,' and rushed out of the cabin toward the bridge. There Moore handed a sealed envelope to the officer of the watch, requesting that it be given to the ship's captain immediately.

History didn't record Captain Herbert J. Haddock's reaction to receiving the news, but if the reaction of his crew is any indication, he likely shared the general sense of shock and confusion. While an experienced captain who had witnessed many times the undeniable power of the sea, 51-year-old Haddock had no reason to doubt what up until now was generally accepted – that White Star's new wonders – *Olympic* and *Titanic* – were impervious to disaster.

Haddock was new to the *Olympic*, having just taken command of her in Southampton in time for her April 3 departure for New York. This was his first eastbound crossing as skipper of the *Olympic*, which was nearly 200 feet longer and 28,000 tons heavier than his previous command, White Star's *Oceanic*.

Perhaps appreciating this fact, White Star Line had given Haddock an extra week to acquaint himself with their new class of liners by putting him in command of the new *Titanic* as she awaited her sea trials. While the ship never left dock during Haddock's tenure, *Titanic* had served as his training ship prior to taking over *Olympic* from White Star commodore E. J. Smith. The two masters exchanged commands on March 30; Smith arrived in Belfast to guide *Titanic* through her day of sea trials while Haddock left to take charge of *Olympic* in Southampton.

Now, Haddock found himself in the very chart room that Smith had left a mere two weeks ago. With the *Titanic*'s position in hand, Haddock worked out the ship's position on a chart and then calculated the distance from his own position, which was 40.52 N, 61.18W. *Olympic* was 500 miles distant from the *Titanic*.

Haddock swung into action to close that gap as quickly as possible. Within 10 minutes of receiving the initial news, *Olympic*'s captain had charted a course for *Titanic* and instructed his chief engineer to pour every ounce of steam into *Olympic*'s engines so that she could make all speed for *Titanic*'s side.

The order to increase speed was carried below decks, where additional crew were awakened to drive the ship as she had never been pushed before. Among them was *Olympic*'s leading fireman.

'We went below and from a speed of 19 knots we soon increased to 23,' he said. 'Men worked as they have never worked before, even to the verge of breaking down.'

Coal had been in short supply, with the most recent coal strike in England ending just days before *Titanic* sailed from Southampton. Other ships' holds had been commandeered by the White Star Line, and that very coal was now powering *Olympic* in her race to *Titanic*'s side.

Haddock and his crew knew they had a great distance to travel. They were also tuning in late to the call for assistance. *Titanic*'s first distress call had been transmitted 35 minutes after the collision at 12:15 a.m., but *Olympic* didn't hear her sister's plea for help for another 25 minutes.

Titanic's first CQD had been heard by *La Provence*, *Frankfurt* and *Mount Temple* and by the land-based station at Cape Race, Newfoundland. *Frankfurt* asked *Titanic* to 'Stand by,' and *Mount Temple*'s operator said he would advise his captain.

Three minutes later, *Ypiranga* heard the distress call as well.

Just 10 minutes later, at 12:25 a.m., *Titanic* was hailed by the Cunard liner *Carpathia*, whose operator, Harold Cottam, had not heard the distress call. Cottam signalled, 'Do you know Cape Cod is sending a batch of messages for you?'

Titanic ignored the question, replying: 'Come at once. We have struck a berg. It's a CQD, OM [old man].' The *Carpathia*, which was less than 50 miles away, asked: 'Shall I tell my captain? Do you require assistance?'

Titanic's answer: 'Yes.'

A minute later, *Titanic* resumed sending a distress call to any station near enough to hear it. With a new position provided by Fourth Officer Boxhall, the ship was now sending, 'Require immediate assistance. We have collision with iceberg. Sinking. Can hear nothing for noise of steam.'

Carpathia returned good news – she was less than 60 miles away and 'coming hard.'

Frankfurt, however, seemed hopelessly out of touch, asking the *Birma*: 'Who is MGY?' *Birma* replies: "MGY is the new White Star liner *Titanic*, old man." Hearing this, *Titanic* gives *Frankfurt* her new position and says, 'Tell your captain to come to our help. We are on the ice.'

Mount Temple came back at 12:30 a.m.: 'Our captain reverses ship. We are about 50 miles off.'

Birma was 100 miles away and wanted to know, 'What is the matter?' She says she will be at *Titanic*'s position at 6:30 a.m.

At 12:34 a.m., *Frankfurt* is back with another question. 'My captain wants to know what's wrong with you.' *Titanic*'s operator, his patience sorely tested after more than 30 minutes of messages to and from an increasingly clueless *Frankfurt*, replies: 'You're a fool! Stand by and keep out.'

Of all the ships to hear *Titanic*'s distress signals by this time, *Olympic* is the most distant from *Titanic*'s position, but as sister ships the two share a strong connection. They were constructed side by side, from the same plans and with the same goal – to be the latest in luxury, comfort and size.

Back in the *Olympic*'s wireless cabin after delivering the initial news to the bridge, chief operator Moore encountered an increasing amount of chatter as more and more wireless stations – both on board ships and on shore – added their voices to the growing clamor of dits and dats now congesting the airwaves above the frigid North Atlantic. In an attempt to break through the noise, Moore signaled 'CQ – QRT' (All stations – stop transmitting). 'This is *Olympic* calling *Titanic*. Stop talking. Stop talking.'

Titanic's reply came at 1:10 a.m.: 'We are in collision with berg. Sinking head down. 41.46 N. 50.14 W. Come soon as possible.' That was immediately followed by a more direct appeal for help: 'Captain says, "Get your boats ready." What is your position?'

At 1:25 a.m., Moore called *Titanic* and transmitted *Olympic*'s position as reported by Haddock. Then he asked, 'Are you steering southerly to meet us?'

Titanic's reply was curt but effective: 'We are putting the women off in the boats.'

While Moore's question had underscored the depth of *Olympic*'s ignorance as to the *Titanic*'s current condition, *Titanic*'s answer conveyed the desperation of her situation in a way that nearly an hour of constant CQDs and SOSs apparently could not.

As if to underscore the point, *Titanic* replied again a moment later: 'We are putting passengers off in small boats.'

Moore had been manning his station alone all this time, but he now decided to wake up the junior operator to assist with the work of transmitting and conveying messages to and from the bridge.

Moore didn't look up but handed an envelope to Bagot, who read the message Moore had scrawled along the outside: 'Commander, *Olympic*. Urgent. The Bridge.'

'It's SOS,' Moore said, not stopping to look up from his work.

Bagot rushed forward to the bridge, where he encountered a few of the ship's officers and her commander, Captain Herbert James Haddock.

Seeing so many officers on the bridge at this hour confirmed to the junior operator that this was really happening.

Bagot handed the envelope to the officer of the watch, who passed it to Capt. Haddock.

Haddock read the latest messages – about the collision with ice and putting the women off in the boats. He then asked the junior operator to follow him to the chart room, where the captain wrote a reply for *Titanic*'s captain.

Haddock made a point of ordering Bagot not to talk about the *Titanic* to anyone. Despite the captain's orders, the veil of secrecy surrounding *Titanic*'s accident had already begun to fall in one first class stateroom because of a perturbed passenger, a mysteriously uncooperative wireless operator and a cabin steward who got caught in the middle.

American architect Daniel H. Burnham, perhaps best known as the man who oversaw the design and construction of the Chicago World's Fair in 1893, was sailing on *Olympic* along with his wife, Margaret, en route to a European vacation.

They had had taken their first meal in the vast First Class Dining Saloon, located one deck below their C-Deck suite, but otherwise had spent much of the voyage thus far in their stateroom. Mr Burnham had suffered from diabetes for the past 15 years, and his feet gave him constant pain.

Perhaps sensing the seriousness of his condition, Burnham had completed his last will and testament just a few days before sailing.[14]

On April 9, the Burnhams had left their Evanston, Illinois, home for Chicago, where they boarded a train for Washington, DC. Mr. Burham's foot pain kept him in his stateroom until the train reached Union Station, one of his crowning achievements as an architect. There he found it necessary to use a wheelchair, which he considered an indignity.

The next day Burnham travelled to the White House for a meeting of the Lincoln Memorial Commission, with President Taft in attendance. The nation's capital was finally getting around to honoring the memory of the sixteenth president, assassinated on April 14–15, 1865. Congress had debated a number of bills since the turn of the century before finally passing a bill in December 1910.

When the meeting concluded, the Burnhams travelled to New York to await *Olympic*'s departure on the 13th. On the eve of departure, Burnham wrote a letter to his old friend and World Fair collaborator, artist Frank Millet, who was travelling with his friend, Col. Archibald Butt, military aide to President William Howard Taft, on board the *Titanic*. The letter, in which Burnham re-hashed the meeting, was left in New York to await Millet's arrival.

> Dear Frank: My wife and I sail to-morrow on the *Olympic* crossing you at sea.
> I am writing this to be handed you on landing ... At the end of the council a vote for designer was about to be taken, but the President deferred until some time next week. I am writing to the President now asking that it be when you can be present, for I feel that the decision is going to be a vital one, settling for a long time the status of the fine arts in this country.[15]

Burnham was aware that *Olympic* and *Titanic* would soon be passing one another in mid-ocean. On the evening of April 14, he wrote a message of greeting to Frank Millet and asked a steward to deliver it to the Marconi office for transmission to the sister ship.[16]

When the steward later returned the un-sent message to Burnham, the architect demanded an explanation.

Faced with the prospect of a disgruntled First Class passenger, the steward made inquiries in the wireless office and by morning was able to offer an explanation: *Titanic* was in trouble, and *Olympic* was racing to her help.

As Mrs Burnham remembered in her diary:[17] 'The steward told us preparations were being made to use the dining hall for hospital, and Mr Burnham offered our rooms for his friends.'

Daniel Burnham took to his diary, too, to record what he had just learned: 'This morning, the steward told us that an accident had occurred on the *Titanic*, sister ship to the one we are on. She sailed from Cherbourg on the 10th.'[18]

If *Olympic* reached *Titanic* in time to rescue the people on board, the Burnhams' friends would have found themselves in familiar territory. Both ships were very similar in nearly every detail. Situated on the *Olympic*'s starboard side, aft of the Grand Staircase, just a few doors beyond the purser's office, the Burnhams' suite, C 63–65, was designed to follow the Louis XVI style with its rich wood paneling embellished by elaborate carvings.

On *Titanic*, Major Butt had a similarly luxurious stateroom, B-38, located just forward of the Grand Staircase on the ship's port side. Butt's room, decorated in the Georgian style, was equally magnificent, and both staterooms shared ocean views through large port windows.

For Francis Millet, transferring to *Olympic* would have been a bit of an upgrade, for his cabin, No. E-38, was three decks below that of his friend Butt, on the lowest deck on *Titanic* to include first class accommodations. Millet's cabin was among the more simple in first class as it was situated near a boiler casing in the corridor aft of the Grand Staircase landing.

It is doubtful that either Millet or Butt was thinking of such accommodations at this hour, however. Both were now engaged in a life-and-death struggle aboard a sinking ship in mid-Atlantic.

CHAPTER 2

'What is the matter with you?'

As the Burnhams were offering their cozy stateroom on board *Olympic* to friends on the *Titanic*, most of *Titanic*'s cabins were already empty, having been abandoned by passengers who had been ordered to leave the warmth of their beds for the bitter cold of *Titanic*'s upper decks.

What had begun as an idyllic maiden voyage the previous Wednesday had quickly turned into a nightmare on this Sunday night.

At 11:40 p.m., just twenty minutes before their watch ended, lookouts Frederick Fleet and Reginald Lee were scanning the sea from *Titanic*'s crow's nest, located about halfway up the forward mast when a dark mass came into their view. It was an iceberg directly in the ship's path. Fleet reached for the brass bell hanging nearby and rang it three times while grabbing the crow's nest telephone. When the officer on the bridge answered the call, Fleet shouted, 'Iceberg right ahead!'

First Officer William Murdoch, who had served on *Olympic* and transferred to *Titanic* along with Captain Smith so that the new ship would have the benefit of his experience with this new breed of super-liner, was officer of the watch on *Titanic*'s bridge. Murdoch didn't hesitate at the moment of crisis, issuing orders immediately in an attempt to avoid the iceberg.

To quartermaster Robert Hichens, who was at the ship's wheel inside the enclosed wheelhouse, Murdoch ordered 'Hard a' starboard!' while using the telegraph to order the engine room to reverse the engines to 'Full speed astern.'

In the seconds that followed, the officers on the bridge and the lookouts in the crow's nest watched anxiously as the great liner raced ahead toward the iceberg that loomed larger with each passing second. At the last moment the ship's bow began the ordered turn toward port, exposing her starboard side to the berg.

As the iceberg reached *Titanic*'s side, the two objects made contact. The liner's immense size meant the collision was felt differently by people on board based on their proximity to the point of impact.

To the lookouts, it seemed to have been 'a close shave' as the ice passed alongside them, depositing large chunks of itself on the deck as it went.

In first class, Lady Lucille Duff Gordon, who usually crossed on the *Lusitania* or 'Luci-tania' as she called it, felt a slight bump 'as though somebody had drawn a long finger along the side of the ship.' Major Arthur Godfrey Peuchen, a yachtsman, thought a large wave had struck the ship. To Madeleine Astor, who was in bed at the time, the event seemed more commonplace – perhaps a mishap in the kitchen.[1]

Farther down, in the third class and crew compartments, the collision was felt more strongly, and its effects were more readily apparent. Lamp trimmer Samuel Hemming was in his bunk at the time of the collision; he heard a strange hissing sound at the forward-most part of the bow, the forepeak. Upon investigating, Hemming realized the sound was caused by air being forced out of the anchor chain locker as water rushed into the compartment.

Third class passengers like Daniel Buckley awakened to find water seeping under their doors and into their cabins. White Star tended to segregate third class men from women and children, so the single men, situated at the bow, were soon carrying their water-logged belongings aft to join the women and children at the stern.

Captain Smith had been resting when the ship struck the berg, but he was on the bridge immediately after Murdoch ordered the watertight doors closed. After learning the ship had struck ice, Smith ordered an inspection of the lower decks forward.

J. Bruce Ismay, chairman of the White Star Line, was on board to experience the *Titanic* as a passenger so that he could conceive of improvements that might be incorporated into the third sister ship, *Gigantic*, which was already under construction.

Having felt the force of the collision, Ismay had stopped only to put a coat over his pajamas and had reached the bridge in time to hear the worst.

It was left to shipbuilder Thomas Andrews, the man who had overseen every phase of construction on the *Titanic*, who knew her better than anyone, to deliver the news.

Summoned to the bridge by Captain Smith after the collision, Andrews learned of the collision and immediately accompanied Smith below decks to inspect the ship's forward-most compartments. The two paused at the entrance to the mail room, now flooding rapidly as the mailmen struggled to move bags of mail to higher ground. The bad news continued as they passed the squash court, which was also filling rapidly.

Devastated by the copious flooding he had just witnessed, the ashen-faced shipbuilder returned to the bridge to explain to Captain Smith and Bruce Ismay that with the five forward-most compartments flooded, *Titanic* was doomed.

Up to this point, Andrews's voyage had been harmonious. When he was not accepting praise for his grand new ship, the shipbuilder was walking about, noting things that could be changed to improve either the form or function of the new steamer.

Along with the other members of the Harland & Wolff guarantee group, all of whom would perish in the sinking, Andrews was making notes to improve not only the *Titanic* but also her sisters, *Olympic* and *Gigantic*.

Before *Titanic* set out from Southampton, members of the ship's crew had presented Andrews with a walking stick to thank him for taking their comfort to heart with the inclusion of such things as a drinking fountain and private restroom for the crew areas.

As Andrews was keenly aware, a more critical accommodation – seats in a lifeboat – were in short supply and many of these same crew members soon would be among the 1,500 people left trapped on the doomed ship.

As the culmination of all their hard work began to slip beneath the waves, Andrews and Ismay struggled to accept the new reality. A few hours ago, Ismay had been preoccupied with the ship's arrival time in New York. Andrews had been noting changes to be made before future crossings, such as reducing the number of screws used to hang each stateroom hat hook.

In one last letter to his wife posted from the ship, Andrews wrote, 'The *Titanic* is now about complete and will I think do the old Firm credit tomorrow when we sail.'

How had it all gone so wrong?

After all the planning and hard work, it had come to this – with Ismay, Andrews and Smith watching the lifeblood drain slowly from their greatest achievement to date.

For most people on *Titanic*, it all came down to fate. Many were former members of *Olympic*'s crew who, until now, considered it an honor to serve on the latest White Star liner.

Among them was Dining Saloon Steward Frederick Ray, who felt a duty to the family of Dr Washington Dodge, who had crossed with him previously on the *Olympic*. As *Titanic* was sinking, the steward noticed Dr Washington Dodge standing on the Boat Deck near lifeboat No. 13. Dodge had already seen his wife and son off in lifeboat No. 5 when the steward urged him into No. 13, saying: 'You better get in here.'[2]

In the same way that *Titanic*'s crew included a large number of old *Olympic* hands, the passenger list for *Titanic*'s maiden voyage included a number of people who had sailed on *Olympic*.

The Astors had fled New York in January on board the *Olympic* when society failed to warm to the new Mrs Astor, and the couple was now returning from a winter spent in Europe (and Egypt). Young Madeleine Astor was expecting a baby in the fall.

Denver millionairess Margaret 'Molly' Brown had sailed with the Astors on *Olympic* when they departed in late January 1912 and was also taking *Titanic* on the return to America.

Known for her hyperbole, Brown nevertheless was quoted by fellow passenger Archibald Gracie in his book, *The Truth about the Titanic*, that as she reached the sea in lifeboat six, she 'looked up and saw the benign, resigned countenance, the venerable white hair, and the Chesterfieldian bearing of the beloved Captain Smith with whom she had crossed twice before, and only three months previous on the *Olympic*. He peered upon those in the boat, like a solicitous father, and directed them to row to the light in the distance – all boats keeping together.'[3]

Harry Widener had made headlines the previous September as one of the wealthy Americans who was inconvenienced when *Olympic*'s voyage to New York was cancelled following her collision with the *Hawke*.

Returning to America with his parents after another winter abroad, Harry would suffer more than inconvenience this time. An avid collector of rare books, he reportedly gave up his seat in a lifeboat in order to retrieve a new book from his cabin and would be among those who died aboard the sinking ship.

Fate must also have been weighing heavily on Major Archibald Butt, who was on board against his will. It was only at the insistence of his friend, Frank Millet, that he had travelled to Europe for a vacation. Butt, 46, had suffered a near breakdown over his conflicting allegiance to both President Taft and Teddy Roosevelt. Only when Millet got a doctor's order and Taft's support did Butt agree to the trip.

Butt had even tried to cancel at the last minute, saying of Taft: 'I really can't bear to leave him just now,' but in the end, Taft convinced his aide to make the trip.[4]

Butt was anxious to be home, even though he soon would have to choose allegiance to either Taft or Roosevelt, and was due to be back in the White House on April 22.

When Millet and Butt boarded *Titanic*, Millet commented on the number of English-Americans on board. 'There are a number of obnoxious, ostentatious American women, the scourge of any place they infest and worse on shipboard than anywhere. Many of them carry tiny dogs, and lead husbands around like pet lambs.'

As the ship's passengers were beginning to appreciate their dangerous predicament, *Titanic's* wireless operators were clearly struggling to convince other ships in her range that the situation was serious.

Captain Smith himself entered the wireless cabin at 12:10 a.m. and, while handing a message with the ship's position to senior wireless operator Jack Phillips, told Phillips to stand by to send out a distress call. A stunned Phillips had only four minutes to ponder the situation before Smith returned with a new order: send the call for assistance immediately.

After the first hour of transmitting their ship's plea for help, senior operator Jack Phillips had convinced the *Olympic*, *Carpathia*, *Mount Temple*, *Birma*, *Baltic* and *Virginian* to proceed to *Titanic's* position, but of these, the majority still had questions about the nature of *Titanic's* injury.

Ships on the way were asking, 'What is the matter with you?'

Even *Olympic* didn't seem to understand. When she asked, 'Are you steering southerly to meet us,' Phillips sent a reply – much more descriptive than anything he'd sent previously: 'We are putting the women off in the boats.'

Then, as if realizing this might illustrate more clearly the seriousness of *Titanic's* situation for all ships, Phillips sends the message again – this time to all stations.

Titanic's crew wasn't having much better luck convincing the passengers to abandon ship, but the confusion was understandable. Claims of unsinkability had spread from shipbuilding publications to the popular press, and the immense *Olympic* and *Titanic*, with their sixteen watertight compartments, seemed to convey invincibility by their sheer size.

The idea for ships of such tremendous size was born of competition and came about during after-dinner conversation in July 1907 at the London home of Lord and Lady Pirrie. Lord Pirrie was the master shipbuilder whose shipyard, Harland & Wolff, had been building ships for the White Star Line for decades. Pirrie's guest that night was J. Bruce Ismay, managing director of the White Star Line.

The shipbuilder and line president were preoccupied by news within the shipping industry. White Star's rival steamship company, Great Britain's Cunard Line, was constructing two steamers that when completed would be the largest and fastest vessels afloat. The first of the two ships, the *Lusitania* (787 feet, 31,550 gross tons), had been launched thirteen months previously, and her sister, *Mauretania* (790 feet, 31,938 gross tons), was launched in September 1906. The news of *Lusitania's* sea trials had made headlines worldwide:

LUSITANIA FINISHED

Glasgow, Sunday. The great Cunard Line turbine steamship *Lusitania* is practically completed. Her official trials will take place on June 27, when the Clyde will be closed to navigation. The *Lusitania* is planned to develop a speed of twenty-five knots. The approach to her landing stage at Liverpool will be deepened to accomodate the vessel.[5]

With the *Lusitania* and *Mauretania*, Cunard would have the biggest steamers in the world, a title previously held by White Star.

Pirrie and Ismay discussed building a class of liners that would surpass the new Cunarders and return White Star to the top of the North Atlantic run.

From their conversation, the idea for *Olympic* and *Titanic* was born.

By 1907, the number of European immigrants entering the United States peaked at more than 1.2 million. That summer, White Star's chairman, and his shipbuilder, decided that they would have to take steps to avoid being eclipsed in the on-going race for domination of the North Atlantic.

Their plans would incorporate key features of Cunard's behemoths – from their long, sleek hulls to their four funnels – but would take the creature comforts of previous White Star liners – including the *Oceanic* – and re-create them on a scale never before seen.

A year after the Pirries' dinner, a contract was signed on July 31, 1908. The Harland & Wolff Shipyard would build the new class of liners.

Only five years earlier, a *Collier's Weekly* editorial had declared that White Star's 700-foot, 21,000 gross ton *Cedric* was 'the largest possible ship':[6]

> Increasing the size and improving the accomodating capacity of the ocean steamships seems to have been fallen back upon by the various companies as the only method of competition, now that the ship combines have become so far-reaching and effective, but it is believed by ship experts that the *Cedric* is the maximum possibility.

Now Harland & Wolff was exceeding the 'maximum possibility' with the construction of 46,000 ton, 882-foot liners. They were on a scale that captured the imagination of the world.

In September, White Star gave names to their new super liners:[7]

OLYMPIC AND *TITANIC*

> London, Sept. 15 - The White Star steamship line has named its two new great liners for the Atlantic service the *Olympic* and *Titanic*.

The Shipbuilder magazine fed the industry's need for information about the new super liners and devoted extensive coverage to Harland & Wolff's new project:

> The builders of the *Olympic* and *Titanic*, the celebrated firm of Harland & Wolff, Limited, have had unrivalled experience in the construction of large passenger vessels, and the new White Star liners but add another triumph to the many which they have to their credit. Unlike many shipbuilding firms, Messrs Harland & Wolff may be termed builders in the most complete sense of the word. As is the case of all vessels built by them, not only have they constructed the hulls of the *Olympic* and

Titanic, but also their propelling machinery, while much of the outfit usually supplied by other yards has been manufactured in their own works.[8]

In order for *Olympic* and *Titanic* to be built side by side, it was necessary for Harland & Wolff to clear space normally used in the construction of three ships. Atop this space the shipyard, in conjunction with Sir William Arrol & Company of Glasgow, Harland & Wolff constructed a massive steel structure called the Arrol Gantry.

Nearly as long as the ships themselves at 840 feet long, the gantry weighed nearly 6,000 tons and rose 228 feet above the shipyard. Equipped with cranes and electric lifts, the gantry would facilitate construction of the biggest ships the world had ever seen.[9] It rose over the shipyard like an enormous steel mountain, and citizens of Belfast could look to it from any vantage point to see the two monster ships taking shape within the Gantry framework.

Olympic would be first to be built and launched, taking 22 months to complete from the moment her keel was laid in December 1908 until her launch in October 1910. *Olympic* was given priority, but work on *Titanic* continued simultaneously, and she was ready after 26 months, having been begun in March 1909 and launched in May 1911.

The plans for *Titanic* began with William Pirrie but soon also involved Pirrie's brother-in-law, Alexander Carlisle, and his nephew, Thomas Andrews.

Andrews studied at the Royal Belfast Academical Institute and sharpened his skills with an apprenticeship at Harland & Wolff. Andrews had been part of the team that built White Star's Big Four – *Celtic*, *Cedric*, *Adriatic* and *Baltic* – and in 1907, he was named managing director and head of the draughting department at Harland & Wolff.

For 35-year-old Andrews, 1908 was a momentous year. He was assigned to oversee the *Olympic* and *Titanic*, his biggest assignment to date, and in June of that year, he married Helen Barbour.

Andrews was well-liked by shipyard workers and clients alike, all of whom admired his laser-like focus and attention to detail.

As the first of White Star's new gigantic liners, *Olympic* captured the imagination of the world. From the time her keel was laid, White Star publicity writers went into action, doling out statistical details about the new ship that were meant to impress a public that had grown accustomed to ever-larger ships. Newspapers were soon filled with details about the scale of the new 'giantess,' as she was often called.

One such anecdote was released in the fall of 1910:

> The rudder of the transatlantic liner *Olympic* weighs 100 tons, being the heaviest ever built.

Unlike *Lusitania* and *Mauretania*, which were built at separate shipyards, *Olympic* and *Titanic* were built side by side and were therefore nearly twins. Any differences between the two were the result of decisions made by the builders to improve upon the first ship by altering the design of the second.

The first hull – that of *Olympic* – was ready for launch in October 1910, and already the press was enthusing about travelling aboard the ship that would not be completed until the following spring.

She Will Make a Big Splash When She is Launched

Want to go abroad? Want to go in the very latest up to datest fashion? Don't go just yet. This year's season is over anyway. Wait until next year and you will be able to cross the ocean in the very latest, biggest, finest of steamers. But get in early your request for accomodations if you want to be one of the first 609 of the first class passengers to cross the ocean from this side to the other in the *Olympic*. There is sure to be a rush for staterooms. No reputation for prophecy is placed in jeopardy when it is stated that the passenger list of the *Olympic* will be full when the big ship sails for the first time for New York from England. Nothing less expressive than slang will do justice to the *Olympic*'s giganticness. So here goes; the *Olympic* will be "some ship" when she is completed. Her owners, the White Star line, might have adhered to their system of giving their vessels names ending with "ic" and might have called her the *Gigantic* were it not for the fact that the *Olympic*'s sister ship, also under construction, is to be named the *Titanic*. *Gigantic* and *Titanic* might sound just a trifle too boastful, even for a big steamship company.[10]

The builders painted *Olympic*'s hull grey above the waterline, making her stand out all the more against the dark framework of the Arrol Gantry and the hull of *Titanic* still under construction in the next slip. They wouldn't do the same for *Titanic*. *Olympic*, as the oldest sister, was the world's first chance to see the new class of liner and was therefore special.

Lord Pirrie and J. Bruce Ismay were among the dignitaries in attendance at the shipyard for the launch on Thursday, October 20. White Star chartered a steamer to bring hordes of journalists to Belfast for *Olympic*'s big day.

Lord Pirrie himself gave the order to launch, and just after 11 a.m. *Olympic* began her slide down the ways and into the water. It was an impressive scene that made headlines worldwide:

BIGGEST STEAMER LAUNCHED

Olympic Exceeds Nearest Rival by 100 Feet and 13,000 Tons.

Belfast, Ireland, Oct. 20 - The first of two mammoth White Star liners, *Olympic* and *Titanic*, was launched successfully amid scenes of enthusiasm today. In accordance with the custom of the White Star Line there was no christening ceremony.[11]

Tugs pulled the *Olympic*'s hull to the nearby outfitting wharf, where shipyard workers, craftsmen and other artisans would spend the next several months adding the machinery, superstructure, equipment and furnishings, etc. that would make her complete.

Work continued on both ships – *Olympic* in the outfitting wharf and *Titanic* still under the enormous Arrol Gantry – through the winter and following spring. For the moment the two ships remained nearly identical. It would only be once *Olympic* was in service that certain improvements would be requested and incorporated into the *Titanic*'s construction.

During outfitting the *Olympic* was fitted with four funnels painted in White Star colors – black on top and buff along the bottom two-thirds. The *Olympic*-class liners required only three funnels, but it was decided to include a fourth 'dummy' funnel so the biggest ship in the world wouldn't have fewer funnels than the *Lusitania* or *Mauretania*.

She was also fitted with a new type of lifeboat davit designed by the Welin Davit & Engineering Company Ltd. The davit made it possible to lower multiple boats from the same davit. After the first lifeboat was lowered, the empty davit arm could be swung inboard to receive and lower another boat.

It was one of many innovations being added to the new ship. Merchants and vendors soon flocked to the shipyard to provide the ship with the thousands of items that she would need to accommodate her full complement of passengers and crew. Vendors whose items were placed on board were soon advertising the fact, thus increasing the publicity being generated by the as-yet unfinished ship.

Olympic's image was soon appearing in ads selling everything from soap to coats and beer.

The public was treated to descriptions of her interiors, and nothing was more alluring than the imagery of her Grand Staircase, one of the greatest symbols of luxury on board:

> We leave the deck and pass through one of the doors that admit us to the interior of the vessel. And, as if by magic, we at once lose the feeling that we are on board a ship, and seem instead to be entering the hall of some great house on shore. Dignified and simple oak paneling covers the walls, enriched in a few places by a bit of elaborate carved work, reminiscent of the days when Grinding Gibbon collaborated with his great contemporary, Wren.
>
> In the middle of the hall rises a gracefully curving staircase, its balustrade supported by light scrollwork of iron with occasional touches of bronze, in the form of flowers and foliage. Above all a great dome of iron and glass throws a flood of light down the stairway, and on the landing beneath it a great carved panel gives its notes of richness to the otherwise plain and massive construction of the wall. The panel contains a clock, on either side of that is a female figure, the whole symbolizing Honour and Glory Crowning Time. Looking over the balustrade, we see the stairs descending to many floors below, and on turning aside we find we may be spared the labour of mounting or descending by entering one of the smoothly gliding elevators which bear us quickly to any other of the numerous floors of the ship we may wish to visit.

The completed *Olympic* was entered into White Star's Liverpool registry on May 25, 1911, and at long last the first of White Star's new super-liners was ready for the sea.

Olympic sailed into Belfast Lough on May 28, 1911 for her sea trials, which as the first ship in her class would take two days. *Titanic*'s trials the following spring would take just one day, the new ship being expected to perform as well as did her older sister.

Olympic returned to Belfast Harbor just in time to witness *Titanic*'s launch.

Summer 1911 truly was the summit for the White Star Line. The shift from speed to spaciousness was now realized in the immense steel hulls of *Olympic* and *Titanic* that towered over the Harland & Wolff shipyard in Belfast.

May 31, 1911 was the biggest red letter day of them all for it marked the delivery of the completed *Olympic* and the launch of *Titanic*.

Pirrie and Ismay were once again on hand for the launch, and once again a horde of reporters were in attendance. White Star hosted them at a lunch following the launch at the Grand Central Hotel in Belfast. The press corps sent a telegram to Lord Pirrie, who was on board *Olympic*, congratulating him on the *Titanic*'s launch and *Olympic*'s successful trials. They also sent birthday wishes to Lord and Lady Pirrie.

At 4:30 p.m. *Olympic* set sail for her home port of Liverpool, where the ship was made available for tours by the general public. White Star had only recently shifted its main port of departure from Liverpool to Southampton, and Ismay insisted on giving Liverpool a chance to enjoy the new liner, too. Funds raised by the public tours were donated to local charities.

Olympic departed Liverpool on the night of April 1, 1911 and arrived in Southampton early on April 3.

J. C. H. Beaumont, who would soon be serving as a doctor on board the new liner, remembered the excitement over *Olympic*'s arrival.

Olympic 'caused a sensation when she first appeared in Southampton ... she looked colossal and even "uncanny" as she towered high above the waterline ... dwarfing all other craft within sight ... To prevent visitors getting lost or strayed, parties had to be formed and led around by guides who were by no means sure of the direct route.'[12]

George Bowyer, the Southampton pilot who would steer *Olympic* and other White Star liners through Southampton waters, also marveled at the new ship's immense size. 'We could hardly believe our eyes there was such a ship!'[13] But Captain Smith, commander of the line's new flagship, seemed undaunted in his reply: 'Yes, but after you have been on board for some time her size will wear off.'

The local press, accustomed to the arrival of the latest achievements in shipbuilding, was equally impressed by *Olympic*, as is evident from this report from the *Southern Daily Echo*:

An unparalleled achievement. Southampton will soon be the home of three *Olympic*-sized ships ... her twin sister *Titanic* will be ready at the end of the year; the third giant has yet to be built, but the triplets will represent £4 1/2 million. The town takes pride in the biggest ships in the world.[14]

Violet Jessop, who would join the new ship as a stewardess in first class, had wondered if the new liner would live up to the hype until the day the big ship arrived in port.

The great day came when *Olympic* finally became a fact, the "largest and finest" to fly the British flag ... She came up to all our expectations and I sensed at once she was going to be a kindly ship, for all ships have a character of their own which some people, more sensitive than others, are quick to realize. That is why there are happy ships, while others have a definitely depressing atmosphere.[15]

CHAPTER 3

'Lighting Up All Possible Boilers'

Olympic and *Titanic* had been born in the same cradle, built from the same plans, by the same men, with the same purpose in mind. So, it stood to reason that the sister ships – and their crews – shared a strong common bond.

Even as *Titanic* lay mortally wounded, the two ships were bound by their sisterly connection. A curious calm had fallen over both ships on the morning of April 15. Neither ship had a public address system, so word of the *Titanic's* peril spread slowly. Had the ships been equipped with such a device, it is doubtful either Captain Smith or Captain Haddock would have used it. Both were determined to avoid panic on their respective ships.

Haddock charted a new course within minutes of receiving *Titanic's* cry for help. More than 500 miles of ocean separated Haddock's ship from *Titanic's* reported position, and he knew he could not reach the scene until sometime the next evening. What he didn't yet know was that, despite *Olympic's* best efforts, it would all be too late. With her sister ship nearly a full day away, *Titanic* had entered the last hour of her life afloat.

Junior wireless operator Bagot returned to *Olympic's* wireless cabin at 1:40 a.m. and handed senior operator Moore the message that Captain Haddock had written for *Titanic's* captain, which Moore transmitted immediately: 'Commander *Titanic*, am lighting up all possible boilers as fast as can. – Haddock.'[1]

In Bagot's absence, Moore had asked *Titanic*, 'What weather have you had?'

'Clear and calm,' was the reply. It was the last direct communication that would flow between the sister ships. With growing frustration, *Olympic's* operators would continue to seek information from *Titanic*, without success.

For their part, *Titanic's* operators weren't arbitrarily ignoring their sister ship's pleas for more information. The fact was she was too far away to help and they knew it. Priority was being given to ships nearer the scene, and the search continued for the elusive ship whose lights could be seen from *Titanic's* decks.

In the absence of news, *Olympic's* wireless operators reviewed what they had learned so far, trying to make sense of the unimaginable. They belatedly observed the changing of their shifts, and Bagot now tuned in to the wireless chatter.

The two men were transfixed by the idea that somewhere in mid-ocean, *Titanic's* passengers were being sent away in lifeboats. They were aware that *Titanic* had asked *Olympic* to have her boats ready, and they knew the reason: neither ship carried enough lifeboats to accommodate everyone on board.

Neither man could convince himself that the *Titanic* was really sinking. In light of the collision, lowering the boats seemed a natural precaution.

Olympic's wireless operators weren't the only people to believe in the unsinkability of *Olympic* and *Titanic*. The belief was widely held until the moment the *Titanic* vanished beneath the waves.

The popular press had reported on the *Olympic*'s unsinkability as early as October 1910, when she was launched:[2]

> In these respects no less than in the matter of mere size the *Olympic* and her sister ship *Titanic* are notable advances on anything now afloat. They are practically unsinkable. Each consists of over thirty watertight compartments [*sic*], and the massive steel doors are all automatically controlled by the officer on the bridge.

Early press reports often included descriptions of the ship's watertight compartments:

> An automatic device on the bridge will control all these heavy steel doors, making it possible for a single hand to close them all in almost an instant in case of danger. Each of these doors will be electrically connected with a chart on the bridge, where each door will be represented by a small electric light, and when one of these doors closes the light will burn red, but while it remains open the disk will be quite dark. The officer on the bridge will thus be able to see at a glance whether or not all the compartments have been closed.[3]

The Shipbuilder, trade publication to the shipbuilding industry, added credibility to the claim in its June 1911 edition, which was devoted to *Olympic* and *Titanic*. The magazine stated: 'The captain may, by simply moving an electric switch, instantly close the watertight doors throughout, making the vessel virtually unsinkable.'

As the world was about to learn in shocking fashion, *Titanic* was far from invincible, but talk of unsinkable ships didn't start with her. Fifty years earlier, a ship called the *Great Eastern* made a much better claim on the concept of unsinkability.

Whereas the *Titanic* and the *Great Eastern* were divided by the same number of transverse or cross bulkheads – fifteen – giving them each sixteen watertight compartments, *Titanic* was 882 feet long compared to *Great Eastern*'s 680 feet. That's where the similarities end.

Great Eastern had two longitudinal bulkheads that ran the length of the ship's machinery space. All told, the *Great Eastern* was in effect divided into fifty separate watertight compartments that were capped at the top as well with a watertight roof.

While *Titanic* had a double bottom, *Great Eastern* had a double skin that covered her bottom and rose to 10 feet above the water line on either side.

Titanic's designers had given her watertight compartments so long as the water didn't reach the top of any given compartment. But without watertight tops, as *Great Eastern* had, water in *Titanic*'s compartments would be free to flow from compartment to compartment if the ship sank low enough, as she did on April 14–15.

But the *Great Eastern*'s design had come at a cost. A ship can't have Grand Staircases that go down numerous decks – or long hallways that lead throughout the ship without interruption – if it's going to truly have watertight compartments with watertight tops. It would be necessary for people to climb out of one compartment and into another to make a ship watertight to the degree of a *Great Eastern*.

Great Eastern's design was put to test when she scraped against rocks on August 26, 1862, off Montauk Point in Long Island Sound. The collision tore a hole 80 feet long and 10 feet wide in the ship's side and bottom, but the ship was able to make it the last 200 miles to New York on her own power. No lives were lost in the incident.[4]

Their faith in *Titanic*'s durability aside, there were things the *Olympic*'s operators didn't yet know.

Just as *Olympic* was hearing *Titanic*'s cry for help for the first time at 12:45 a.m., *Titanic* was lowering her first lifeboat – No. 7 – from the starboard side. At the same time, the first distress rocket was fired from the deck of the sinking ship.

While only twenty-eight of a possible sixty-five people saw fit to board lifeboat No. 7, the rocket was an ominous sign, as second class passenger Lawrence Beesley observed.

> … if there were any one who had not by now realized that the ship was in danger, all doubt on this point was to be set at rest in a dramatic manner. Suddenly a rush of light from the forward deck, a hissing roar that made us all turn from watching the boats, and a rocket leapt upwards to where the stars blinked and twinkled above us. Up it went, higher and higher, with a sea of faces upturned to watch it, and then an explosion that seemed to split the silent night in two, and a shower of stars sank slowly down and went out one by one. And with a gasping sigh one word escaped the lips of the crowd: "Rockets!" Anybody knows what rockets at sea mean.[5]

At the same time, Captain Smith ordered lifeboat No. 4 to be lowered from the Boat Deck to A Deck and loaded from there. An alert First Class passenger named Hugh Woolner reminded the captain that unlike *Olympic*, the forward portion of A Deck on *Titanic* is enclosed with glass screens. 'Have you forgotten, sir,' Woolner asked, 'that all those glass windows are closed?'

Realizing his mistake, Captain Smith replied, 'By God, you are right!' and ordered that boat No. 4 and the passengers waiting to board it should be returned to the Boat Deck.[6] That wasn't the end of the confusion, however. The glass screens eventually were removed, and passengers passed through the window openings to board Boat 4, one of the last to leave the ship.

At 1 a.m., when *Titanic* was first informing *Olympic* that 'We have struck an iceberg,' the water had just reached the foot of *Titanic*'s grand staircase on E deck. From that moment on, *Titanic* passengers who peered down the staircase from the railing would be able to watch *Titanic*'s rate of decline by the time it took the green sea water to creep up the stairs, step after step, flight after flight, deck after deck.

When *Olympic* last contacted *Titanic* directly, at 1:40 a.m., to let her know the *Olympic* was 'lighting up all possible boilers as fast as can,' the last of *Titanic*'s distress rockets was soaring into the sky. At the same time, the sea began to pour into the forward well deck.

From *Titanic*'s sparse messages sent thus far, it was possible to read between the lines and find hope. After 1:40 a.m., *Olympic* never again heard directly from *Titanic*. But messages continued to pour in from other ships nearer the scene – sometimes with helpful information.

At 1:45 a.m., *Carpathia* heard from *Titanic* for the last time: 'Engine room full up to boilers.' At the same time, *Mount Temple* heard *Frankfurt* calling *Titanic* with no reply.

A few minutes later, *Caronia* heard *Titanic* signaling, but the message was unintelligible. *Asian* heard an SOS but was unable to get a response.

At 1:50 a.m., *Olympic* transmitted to all ships that she was 'Going to assistance of *Titanic*.'

In the absence of new information, ships began to report what they'd heard, sometimes offering speculation to explain *Titanic*'s silence.

The wireless station at Cape Race, Newfoundland, had been monitoring the messages since the first CDQ came through, and at 1:55 a.m. added its voice to the list of stations speculating about *Titanic*'s condition. 'We have not heard *Titanic* for about half an hour. His power may be gone.'

Not quite. *Titanic*'s operators, Phillips and Bride, continued signaling even as their power to transmit or receive messages faded. Just after 2:05 a.m., with *Titanic* sinking faster now, Captain Smith entered the wireless cabin for the last time.

'Men, you have done your full duty,' Smith said. 'You can do no more. Abandon your cabin. Now it's every man for himself.'[7]

Phillips remained at his work, and the Captain once again urged them to leave. 'You look out for yourselves. I release you. That's the way of it at this kind of time.'

Smith left the room, but Phillips remained at his set. At 2:17 a.m., *Virginian* heard *Titanic* call 'CQ.' The signal ended abruptly, as though the power had suddenly been switched off.

As Phillips continued to tap away at the wireless key, junior operator Bride returned from the cabin where he'd retrieved his money. Bride discovered a stoker who was quietly trying to remove and steal Phillips's life jacket. The wireless operators joined forces against the stoker, knocking him unconscious. The two then abandoned their cabin, joining the hundreds of people now struggling along *Titanic*'s sloping decks.

No more messages would come from *Titanic*, which lost power for good some time after 2:15 a.m. For the next 5 minutes, the 1,500 people left stranded on her decks, or in the freezing water below, struggled to save themselves as their ship made her final plunge.

At 2:20 a.m., *Titanic* vanished beneath the waves, leaving a halo of smoke that hung in the air above her last position like a grave marker.

At that moment, *Olympic*'s wireless operators were listening for any word from the sister ship.

Even now, when a series of ominous messages had ended in silence, Bagot and Moore remained hopeful that they would reach the ship in time to save lives. 'If *Titanic* had sustained heavy damage, passengers, doubtless, would want to be transferred to her sister ship, possibly taken in her to New York. Hence the message, "Get your boats ready," for neither *Titanic* nor *Olympic* carried lifeboat accommodations for more than forty percent of the complement.'

Remarkably, many of *Titanic*'s passengers and crew held the same hope: that *Olympic* soon would be arriving to rescue them, even after *Titanic* was gone.

Lawrence Beesley was among the survivors who would later recall hearing of only one ship when talk turned to rescue: *Olympic*.

'Our plan of action was simple, to keep all the boats together as far as possible and wait until we were picked up by other liners,' Beesley said. 'The crew had apparently heard of the wireless communications before they left the *Titanic*, but I never heard them say that we were in touch with any boat but the *Olympic*; it was always the *Olympic* that was coming to our rescue. They thought they knew even her distance, and making a calculation, we came to the conclusion that we ought to be picked up by her about two o'clock in the afternoon. But this was not our only hope of rescue.'[8]

As Beesley recalled, 'A stoker said, "The sea will be covered with ships tomorrow afternoon; they will race up from all over the sea to find us." Some even thought that fast torpedo boats might run up ahead of the *Olympic*.'

For the moment, however, *Olympic* was still hundreds of miles away. While *Titanic*'s passengers and crew continued to hope the sister ship would come to save them, neither the two ships nor their masters were destined to meet again.

Fate had intersected with many lives here, starting with two White Star captains – H. J. Haddock and E. J. Smith – whose paths had last crossed just a few short weeks ago in Belfast, where they assumed their new commands.

For a week in late March, Haddock had been summoned to Belfast for a brief introduction to the new class of steamers for which he was about to assume a command. He was made master of the *Titanic* during her last week at Harland & Wolff. Perhaps White Star felt that such an initiation might be helpful to the skipper who was leaving the 17,272-gross ton *Oceanic* in order to command the 45,324-gross ton *Olympic*.

Haddock signed on as master of the *Titanic* on Wednesday, March 25, just in time to oversee her final Board of Trade inspection, undertaken while the vessel was still docked at the Queen's Island yard. *Titanic*'s anchors and her sixteen lifeboats under davits were inspected and deemed passable.

The next day, Haddock was in command when the first of *Titanic*'s senior crew reported for duty in a party that included Joseph G. Boxhall, Herbert J. Pitman, Harold G. Lowe and James P. Moody. Moody and Pitman were familiar faces, having served under Haddock on *Oceanic*.

As Moody wrote at the time: 'Daddy Haddock is going to the *Olympic* until old "E. J." retires on his old age pension from the *Titanic*.'[9]

Haddock's duties on *Titanic* were mostly supervisory as he awaited the arrival of Captain Smith, who would replace him as *Titanic*'s master while Haddock would assume command of Smith's last charge, the RMS *Olympic*.

On Friday, March 29, Haddock continued to oversee the mustering of *Titanic*'s crew as seventy-nine firemen and stokers signed on to the new ship for her upcoming sea trials and subsequent voyage to Southampton. The notoriously publicity-shy captain was no doubt less enthusiastic about another duty that day – to welcome a special party, comprising mostly journalists, who were invited aboard to inspect the new *Titanic* before she departed Belfast.

On Sunday, March 31, Haddock got a chance – albeit it a short-lived one – to experience the power of the *Olympic* class for himself when he swung *Titanic* around to face the sea on the eve of her sea trials.

The next day brought disappointment. High winds forced a postponement of the trials just as Captain Smith arrived to take over command of the line's new flagship.

Just as quickly as it had begun, Haddock's introduction to the immense new *Olympic* class of liners – seven days on a ship that never left harbor – was over, and he was off to Southampton, where his 882.5-foot command awaited: RMS *Olympic*.

As *Titanic* proved her seaworthiness through a day of trials, Haddock was busy acquainting himself with the *Olympic* as preparations were being made for her next departure on April 3.

On April 2, *Titanic* spent about 12 hours in Belfast Lough and the Irish Sea before returning to Belfast, where the Board of Trade certified the new liner. Just after 8 p.m., *Titanic* left Belfast bound for Southampton a week in advance of her long-awaited maiden voyage.

Scores of old *Olympic* hands awaited the arrival of their new ship, *Titanic*, to which they transferred. Meanwhile, *Olympic* departed Southampton at noon on Wednesday, April 3 for her first voyage under the command of her new master, H. J. Haddock, and a complement of crew that was largely unfamiliar with the grand size and scale of so large a ship.

That evening the westbound *Olympic* passed *Titanic*, still en route from Belfast to Southampton, in what was the last time the two sister ships would ever meet. Shortly after midnight, *Titanic* steamed into Southampton harbor and was eased into the White Star dock just vacated by her older sister.

The next day, Southampton awakened to the sight of the new liner *Titanic* – not unlike the *Olympic* – but exciting nonetheless as the next 'big un.'

CHAPTER 4

'Well Known to White Star Travelers'

The two principal characters in the events of April 14–15, 1912, were men of similar experience at sea who, despite their differences in personal style and temperament, had loyally served the White Star Line for many years.

Herbert J. Haddock didn't court publicity as enthusiastically as did his fellow White Star captain, Edward J. Smith. In fact, Haddock was noted for going out of his way to avoid publicity. Through his years of service to the line, however, he had become just as familiar and welcome a sight on a steamer's bridge as Smith.

With his jovial laugh, his penchant for good conversation and an after-dinner cigar, and his resemblance to the late King Edward VII, which was so strong it seemed deliberate, Smith became known as the 'millionnaire's captain.' He was immensely popular among the wealthy passengers who made a point of travelling on his ships.

Haddock, who was described as being the only captain on the Atlantic with the old-fashioned mutton chops, was also a popular, if less gregarious, captain.

As stewardess Violet Jessop would recall,

> Our commander, Captain Haddock, was himself a Royal Navy man, a lovable character and a true English gentleman of the old school. His unpretentious appearance, quiet manners, old-fashioned side whiskers and a coachman's top coat when ashore, often caused landsmen to mistake his calling. He loved to relate such incidents to the passengers at his table, chuckling softly with one eyebrow whimsically raised.[1]
>
> To a stranger, perhaps the attraction of this rather unprepossessing man lay in his charming and restful voice, probably the result of generations of good breeding, and his steadfast eyes. When surprised, they would widen into a questioning, slightly bewildered stare and, without a word, he would turn to whoever was with him and invariably scratch the top of his head with a sort of childish perplexity. But to us all, the thing that drew our unquestioning loyalty was his naturalness and his intensely human manner of dealing with his fellow men.

Both Smith and Haddock had heeded a calling to the sea at a young age.

Ten years older than Haddock, Smith was born January 17, 1850. He came to Liverpool at thirteen for training as a seaman; Haddock would do the same at age fourteen, when he entered Cadet College.

In 1869, Smith served as an apprentice on board the *Senator Weber*, an American clipper ship, and joined the square-rigged *Lizzie Fennel* on the South American run in 1876.

Smith joined the White Star Line in March 1880 as fourth officer of the old *Celtic*, a 437-foot, 3,800 ton single-screw vessel with four masts and a single funnel.

Haddock's first command for the line was the 5,000-ton *Britannic*. The 468-foot liner, which entered service in June 1874, was built during the transition from sailing ships to steam, and like many ships of this era her design included funnels (two) and masts (four) for sailing.

Early in her career *Britannic* was perhaps best known for two events – one happy and the other calamitous.

In 1876, the *Britannic* won for White Star the coveted Blue Riband, an award given to the ship that crossed the Atlantic at the highest rate of speed, with an average speed of more than 15 knots for both a westward and eastward crossing.

The *Britannic* and her sister, *Germanic*, were built for speed. Other White Star liners would win the Blue Riband, but after the *Britannic/Germanic*, White Star never purposefully designed ships to win the prize, choosing to focus instead on ships build for comfort and luxury.

The other incident occurred on May 19, 1887 when the eastbound *Britannic* collided with White Star's westbound *Celtic* in thick fog about 350 miles east of Sandy Hook, New Jersey. Twelve people died on *Britannic*, while *Celtic* didn't suffer any casualties. Neither ship was lost and both made it back to New York harbor with help from other vessels.

Haddock's command came later in *Britannic*'s career, but his time as skipper wasn't without memorable incidents.

Two days out of Liverpool on a westbound crossing, *Britannic* slowed down about 8 a.m. on April 20, 1896 to avoid a field of large icebergs that would stretch over the next 130 miles. At 10 a.m. the ship was suddenly struck by an enormous wave that swept over the bridge, which Captain Haddock had just left. The rogue wave shattered the starboard lifeboat to pieces and nearly swept First Officer Chapman overboard. Nobody was killed in the incident, but some steerage passengers suffered bruises as they were tossed about the deck.[2]

Bad weather and rogue waves were not uncommon on the North Atlantic run – particularly in the month of April – and three years later *Britannic* again encountered the worst of it.

When the ship arrived in Queenstown on April 21, 1899, Haddock reported having endured heavy seas that made it impossible for his ship to communicate with shore.[3]

The previous year, *Britannic*'s captain and crew found themselves engaged in a more human drama involving theft of mail being transported by the steamer.[4]

In August 1898, four members of *Britannic*'s crew were arrested on smuggling charges in connection with a plot to steal bonds from mail packages in the hold. Captain Haddock met with an Assistant US District Attorney along with assistant steward Henry Galway, who confessed to his role in the plot.

'There is no doubt in my mind that a robbery of the mails has been committed about the *Britannic*,' said Postmaster Van Cott. 'The robbers must have broken the seal and repaired it so neatly that it escaped detection. I know the seals were closely examined when the *Britannic*'s mail was received, and they were found apparently untouched.'

It was estimated that the bonds, when matured, would be worth more than $20,000.

Haddock's next post was *Britannic*'s twin, *Germanic*, which entered service in May 1875. She, too, had twice won the Blue Riband for White Star – in February 1876, and again in August 1877.

Just before Haddock assumed command, *Germanic* underwent a major refit that was necessitated by an accident that befell her on February 13, 1899 under Captain E. R. McKinstry's command. While docked in New York harbor, the ship became so covered by snow and ice that she was pulled under, sinking where she was docked. Ten days later, she was refloated and returned to Harland & Wolff for a complete overhaul.

It was in this new condition that Haddock inherited *Germanic*. Like her sister, *Britannic*, before her, bad weather in mid-ocean dogged *Germanic* from time to time. In March 1901, she was reported overdue in New York. Two days late, she finally appeared through a dense fog at Sandy Hook, where she was forced to anchor for the night given the lack of visibility.

Explaining her tardiness when *Germanic* docked the next day, Haddock said the ship had encountered stormy weather, with gales so strong that the ship could only proceed at half speed.[5]

Haddock received good news in August 1902 when his ship reached Liverpool. England's King Edward VII, for which the Edwardian Age got its name, had just named Haddock a Commander of the Bath, an honor often afforded members of the military (including the Royal Navy) on special occasions, such as the Coronation, which for Edward took place that same month.[6]

Having proven himself a reliable and popular skipper among passengers and peers, Haddock was about to receive a new command that would elevate him to the top of White Star's roster.

RMS *Cedric*, completed in 1903, was the flagship of White Star's fleet and, at the time, the largest ship afloat. With this ship, Harland & Wolff and White Star took another step toward the super liners that would culminate in the ships of the *Olympic* class.

Cedric was not only the largest ship afloat; she was also one of the first ships in history to exceed the immense size of the famous 692-foot *Great Eastern*, which for nearly 40 years had dwarfed all other craft on the high seas. The 700-foot *Cedric* was a 21,000-ton, twin-funneled vessel that could achieve a maximum speed of 16 knots.

As captain of the *Cedric*, Haddock would for the first time experience the excitement of taking a new ship out on her maiden voyage – commanding for the first time the flagship of the line. Shortly before her maiden departure for America, *The New York Times* reported on what New Yorkers could expect to see when the newest ship arrived:[7]

There are nine decks on the *Cedric*. She is built on the cellular double bottom principle, and has numerous water-tight compartments that make her practically unsinkable. She has four masts and, like all the other great White Star liners, two massive buff funnels ...

With the completion of the *Cedric*, the White Star Line gains the distinction of owning the two largest vessels in the world, and the additional distinction of owning thirteen vessels exceeding 10,000 tons each. The commander of the *Cedric* will be Lieut Haddock, R.N.R., who is well known to White Star travelers.

Her maiden voyage from Liverpool to New York began on February 11, 1903 and ended without incident on February 21. *The New York Times* reported on the first arrival of the grand new steamer:[8]

The largest steamship ever constructed slowly made her way, last evening between 6 and 8 o'clock, up New York Bay and the North River to the White Star piers at the foot of Banks Street. The huge vessel was the new transatlantic liner *Cedric*, a sister of the *Celtic* of the same fleet, but ninety-six tons larger.

Cedric was a popular addition to what would become known as White Star's 'Big Four,' four steamers built for luxury and comfort, intended to be more blue ribbon than Blue Riband. Her elder sister, *Celtic*, had entered service in 1901. Two ships of even greater size – *Baltic* and *Adriatic* – were to follow in 1903 and 1907 respectively. These four ships were to dominate the North Atlantic run until the advent of Cunard's great super liners, *Mauretania* and *Lusitania*.

A year after *Cedric*'s maiden voyage, E. J. Smith commanded *Baltic* as she departed Liverpool on her maiden voyage on June 29, 1904. On board was J. P. Morgan, the American financier whose International Mercantile Marine combine owned a number of shipping companies, including the White Star Line.[9]

There were misgivings about the building of ships so large that, as in case of *Celtic* and *Cedric*, harbors had to be dredged to be deep enough to accommodate the immense new ships.

In an editorial offered in April 1903 that would soon seem hopelessly out of touch, *Collier's Weekly* declared that *Cedric* was surely the biggest ship that would be possible to construct:[10]

Cedric, the Largest Possible Ship.

By passing onward from larger size to larger size, the transatlantic ship companies have finally reached what is deemed by many observers to be the limit in ship expansion. In the new ship of the White Star line, the *Cedric* – which made its first appearance in New York harbor in the latter part of February, ice-clad and ponderous, after a maiden voyage from England – a capacity is afforded for over twenty-six hundred passengers, in addition to a crew of three hundred and thirty-five. The decks of the vessel rise above the water more or less like stories of a hotel, and newspaper artists, seeking for some means of conveying an adequate impression of the ship's size, have drawn it to scale with the great Flatiron building in New York – with a result not flattering to the building. Increasing the size and improving the accommodating capacity of the ocean steamships seems to have been fallen back upon by the various companies as the only method of competition, now that the ship combines have become so far-reaching and effective, but it is believed by ship experts that the *Cedric* is the maximum possibility.

The new emphasis on size may have cost White Star any claim to the Blue Riband speed records, but the line gained accolades from passengers and crew alike for the new steadiness experienced on liners of the increased beam and breadth.

Newfoundland governor Sir Cavendish Boyle sailed on *Cedric* in March 1903 and upon arriving in New York was full of praise for the new ship,[11] declaring her as steady as a rock even as high seas slammed into her sides. 'The *Cedric*,' he said, 'is a good example of the kind of ships the Morgan combine is turning out.'

A veteran White Star smoke room steward identified only as Clegg shared with reporters the results of an experiment he conducted on board ship that proved her steadiness.

'When we left Queenstown, I placed a small white wine glass filled with champagne on the edge of a sideboard on the port side of the smoke room,' Clegg said. 'I never touched that glass all the way across, and when we got to Sandy Hook to-day the glass had not moved half an inch and not a drop of wine had been spilled. Now, that proves that the *Cedric* is a wonder, doesn't it?'

If anyone among the travelling public had misgivings about travelling on so large a ship, *Cedric*'s surgeon, Dr R. D. Dole, said that none of the passengers was seasick, even when *Cedric* encountered high seas and gales.

'They did not bother us any, though,' agreed Captain Haddock, 'for on this ship you would hardly know you were at sea unless you happened to take a walk on the deck or looked out of your stateroom window.'

Indeed, Haddock had noted *Cedric*'s steadiness upon her first return to Liverpool, declaring the new vessel 'steady as a church.'[12]

It was smooth sailing for Haddock and *Cedric* until November 1903, when an ominous rumor originating in Liverpool soon spanned the globe:[13]

Cedric is Sunk

Collision in Midocean With Smaller Steamer is Rumored

New York, Nov. 26 – A rumor which has been certied and the source of which cannot be traced is current that the White Star liner *Cedric* has been in a collision with a Lamport & Holt liner in mid-Atlantic, and that the *Cedric* has sunk with all on board.

The rumor is nowhere credited, but friends of those aboard the *Cedric* are anxiously awaiting her arrival in New York. She is due today. The *Cedric* sailed from Liverpool last Wednesday with 290 first-class passengers, 160 second-class and 540 steerage passengers.

In an eerie echo of a disaster set to unfold in less than nine years, White Star officials found themselves besieged by worried relatives of passengers on a White Star vessel rumored to have sunk in mid-ocean overnight.

White Star officials were confident in their ship's durability, as evidenced by the statement issued by General Manager John Lee:

I do not believe the *Cedric* has met with any such disaster. The *Cedric* has more water-tight compartments than any other ship in the world. I do not believe she could be sunk. Her compartments can be closed in fifteen seconds. If she should be cut in half a dozen pieces, each piece ought to float.

White Star officials studied maps of the North Atlantic and reasoned that the ships would not have come in contact with one another.[14]

We have no ground whatever for placing the slightest credence in the reported sinking of the *Cedric* in midocean. We deny it absolutely. It is simply a cruel hoax, and all efforts to trace it to its origin have failed. We expect that the *Cedric* will be reported to-night or to-morrow morning.

Soon the other ship involved in the rumored collision, the Lamport & Holt steamship *Titian*, arrived in Manchester, where her crew denied having been involved in any accident at sea. On the evening of the 26th, *Cedric* arrived at her New York City pier to an enthusiastic greeting from a large crowd of well-wishers.

By the time Cedric docked, *The New York Times* had already published its belief that *Cedric* had not been lost:[15]

The *Cedric* is by several thousand tons the largest ship now in the water. She made her maiden voyage in February, since which time she has not met with a single accident. She has the greatest number of water-tight compartments of any ship afloat, which are believed to render her almost practically unsinkable.

In its editions on the following Sunday, *The New York Times* printed an explanation for its coverage of what turned out to be a rumor.[16]

Our regret, already expressed, that the rumors as to the loss of the *Cedric* were put in circulation should not be interpreted as acquiescence in the too common opinion that the newspapers are always publishing sensational stories, only to contradict them the next day, and that one can never trust what one sees in the newspapers.

The report about the *Cedric*, or, rather, the news that such a report had been put in circulation in Liverpool, was just as much news, and just as legitimate news, as any that a paper could print. It was a fact about which there was no question whatever, and the only duty of the papers was to present it for exactly what it was worth. This they did, so far as we have noticed, in no case attempting to give the story a value it did not possess or to excite unnecessary fears. The circumstance that the story was in all probability false was not concealed; it was, on the contrary, emphasized, and when the *Cedric* steamed calmly into port the newspapers hastened to allay the fears that had been aroused, not by themselves, but by mysterious persons who probably had no ill-intentions in what they did and only distributed unintentionally exaggerated deductions from misunderstood information.

Cedric was safe and sound – but this wouldn't be the last time White Star officials and Captain Haddock would find themselves trying to confirm what appeared to be wild rumors in the middle of the night.

Two years later, *Cedric* encountered the worst storm of her career, as *The New York Times* reported on March 21, 1905:[17]

GREAT WAVES SMASH *CEDRIC*'S DECKWORK

Most of the belated and storm-beaten transatlantic liners got in yesterday, the fleet being led by the White Star giant *Cedric* from Liverpool, while the Cunarder *Lucania*, which docked late into the afternoon, was the last.

The *Cedric* was eleven days in making the passage, and her commander, Capt. Haddock, declared the voyage one of the most remarkable in his long experience. Her log shows that in the early morning of last Wednesday, in mid-ocean, she was boarded in rapid succession by three great waves, the like of which are seldom seen on the Atlantic.

According to the ship's log, waves cresting at sixty feet high struck *Cedric* – first on her port bow, which caused the ship to roll heavily to starboard. A second wave destroyed a hatch cover, part of the port rail and several lights on the port side. The final wave bent several of the ship's steel plates.

Cedric endured the storm and finally arrived in port on March 20. During the worst part of the storm, a steerage passenger named Sarah Whitney gave birth to a son, whom she named Cedric.

Births on board ship were not uncommon. The following June, a steerage passenger gave birth while crossing on the *Baltic*, which was under Captain Smith's command.[18]

Steerage passenger Nellie Frawley of New Britain, Connecticut, died on June 26, 1906 while giving birth to triplets, each of which also died within hours of their birth. A burial service was conducted that evening by the ship's purser as the bodies were buried at sea.

When the ship reached New York, Captain Smith couldn't bring himself to break the sad news to Nellie's husband, who was waiting at the pier.

Yesterday morning the husband of Mrs Frawley was at the pier to meet her when the liner docked. None of the passengers could gather courage to break the news to him, and finally the purser was delegated by the Captain to tell him that his wife and babies were dead. Frawley broke down utterly. He went on board, got his wife's baggage and, still weeping as if his heart would break, he left the pier.

Just months later, White Star's *Oceanic* encountered yet another storm in November 1906 while steaming from Southampton to New York. Her captain, James G.

Cameron, was knocked off his feet when a huge wave swept across the bridge, and Cameron was rendered unconscious. Cameron was treated by the ship's doctor and returned to the bridge to guide his ship into port.

Cameron had been *Oceanic*'s master since her maiden voyage on September 6, 1899, but in April 1907 he accepted a new post as White Star's superintendent in Southampton. Haddock left *Cedric* at this time to assume command of the *Oceanic*, which at 17,272 gross tons and 704 feet in length was slightly smaller than *Cedric*. Often described as one of the most beautiful liners of the new century, *Oceanic*'s design incorporated her bridge into the superstructure rather than the separate 'island' bridge that was a feature of *Celtic* and *Cedric*. At her launch *Oceanic* was the world's largest ship. She was never intended to compete for the Blue Riband, but was instead built as part of White Star's new emphasis on comfort and luxury.

Oceanic was then known as Queen of the Seas, as Charles Lightoller, who would serve as *Oceanic*'s first officer, would recall in his memoir, *Titanic and other Ships*:[19]

A wonderful ship, built in a class of her own, and by herself. The usual custom is to build twin ships, as with *Britannic* and *Germanic*, *Teutonic* and *Majestic*. Then, in lone and stately majesty came the *Oceanic*. She was an experiment, and a wonderfully successful one; built by Harland & Wolff, regardless of cost, elaborate to a degree, money lavished where it was necessary, but never gaudily as is so common nowadays. Her smoke room doors were a masterpiece in themselves, and cost £500.

Captain Smith commanded the new 729-foot, 24,000-ton *Adriatic*, the fastest and biggest of White Star's big four, as she made her maiden arrival in New York City in May 1907.[20] On the occasion of her maiden arrival, Smith spoke to reporters about his experiences at sea.

When any one asks me how I can best describe my experiences of nearly 40 years at sea I merely say, "uneventful." Of course, there have been winter gales and storms and fog and the like, but in all my experience I have never been in an accident of any sort worth speaking of. I have seen but one vessel in distress in all my years at sea, a brig, the crew of which was taken off in a small boat in charge of my third officer. I never saw a wreck, and have never been wrecked, nor was I ever in any predicament that threatened to end in disaster of any sort.

The love of the ocean that took me to sea as a boy, has never left me. In a way, a certain amount of wonder never leaves me, especially as I observe from a bridge a vessel plunging up and down in the trough of the sea, fighting her way through and over great waves. A man never outgrows that.

Smith went on to say that modern shipbuilding had reached such a level that disaster was unthinkable.

'I will go a bit further,' he said. 'I will say that I could not imagine any condition that could cause a ship to founder. I cannot conceive any vital disaster happening to this vessel. Modern shipbuilding has gone beyond that.'

A month after Smith's statement, Haddock was slightly more than a year into his tenure on *Oceanic*'s bridge when the liner was victim of a fire that broke out on Monday, June 2, 1907, while she was docked in New York.[21]

LINER *OCEANIC* AFIRE AT HER PIER

Stubborn Blaze Breaks Out Shortly Before 2 o'clock This Morning

Shortly before 2 o'clock this morning fire was discovered in the steerage of the White Star liner *Oceanic*, which was docked at the foot of West Eleventh Street. Officers and members of the crew of the steamboat being unable to cope with the blaze with water obtained from the pier, sent in an alarm.

When the fire apparatus arrived lines of hose were stretched from West Street and two fireboats started to work. The blaze proved to be a stubborn one.

A crewman discovered the fire and sounded an alarm after he saw smoke billowing out of the steerage section of the ship. Captain Haddock ordered men below decks to fight the blaze, and fire hoses were soon scattered along *Oceanic*'s decks.

The fireboat *McClellan* was soon alongside and helped fight the fire, which was under control by 2.45 a.m. *Oceanic*'s steerage quarters suffered extensive damage, totaling more than $10,000. It could have been much worse had passengers been aboard, but the blaze occurred between voyages.

The following year, Captain Smith and the *Adriatic* made headlines for smoke of another kind when a group of women in first class decided to smoke cigarettes in public rooms on board ship – something that was considered quite taboo at the time.

As *The Washington Post* reported when the ship reached New York on Jan. 26, 1908:

Smoke rolled in pretty rings from the rosy lips of many women on board the White Star liner *Adriatic* during the trip from Southampton to this port ... They flicked the ashes with a nonchalance that delighted the men passengers. And even the women on board who did not puff cigarettes forgot to make remarks.[22]

The ship was two days outbound from Cherbourg when Lady Juliet Duff, daughter of the fourth Earl of Lonsdale, and the Hon. Violet Mary Vivian, sister of Baron Vivian and maid of honor to the Queen, lit up cigarettes while relaxing in the lounge after dinner. Soon, other women followed suit.

Those women who smoked but who took care not to let any one see them, stood hesitatingly for a moment, but only for a moment. Then they caught up their skirts, and away they went to their staterooms. There they seized their cigarettes, and then back to the lounge they went. Matches went off like a bunch of firecrackers, and all kinds of cigarettes appeared between the lips of a dozen women – cigarettes with gold tips, silver tips, and plain tips, some monogrammed, and some not.

In five minutes no one would have known from the looks of those women smokers that anything out of the ordinary had happened. They puffed and puffed, and between puffs remarked.

"Wretched weather, isn't it?"

Sometimes they would punctuate a sentence with a puff, so proficient were they in the art. Some of the passengers, the ones, of course, who were amateurs in the ways of the world, were horrified at first, but before they could express their thoughts they decided that perhaps it wasn't so horrible, after all.

A year later, Haddock was bringing the *Oceanic* over from Southampton when, on Saturday, January 2, 1909, she lost a blade on her port propeller.[23] Losing a propeller blade at sea, when the ship is at full steam, can cause severe damage if the ship is not slowed down immediately. On *Oceanic* the passengers were at dinner when the blade was dropped, which caused quite a tremble throughout the ship.

Haddock was able to guide his ship to New York, but was further delayed by dense fog as she approached the Nantucket Lightship on Wednesday, June 6. She didn't reach her New York pier until the following day.

On November 24, 1909, Haddock received good news via cable from London. King Edward had conferred officers' decorations of the British Royal Navy Reserve upon him and three of his White Star peers – Commander Bertram Hayes of *Laurentic*, Commander Benjamin Steel, who was then Marine Superintendent at Liverpool, and Lt J. E. Crossland, of White Star's Australian service.[24]

A year later almost to the day, *Oceanic* was involved in a collision in New York harbor that sent a coal barge to the bottom:[25]

OCEANIC SINKS COAL BARGE

Captain of Small Craft and His Wife Escape in Peculiar Manner.

New York, Nov. 23 – When the White Star liner *Oceanic*, in from Southampton, was coming up the bay today, under reduced speed, she ran into a barge laden with coal and sent it to the bottom. The skipper of the barge, Capt. Herman Coutant, and his wife were in the cabin when the crash came, and their lives were saved because of the quick inrush of water through the gaping wound in the barge's side, which forced the couple up through the companionway and into the bay, where they were picked up.

The barge, which was in tow of the tug *Huntington*, was caught in a strong ebb tide, and she failed to clear the *Oceanic*'s bow. Hundreds of passengers on the *Oceanic* witnessed the collision.

Lightning struck *Oceanic* again – quite literally this time – during a westbound crossing. On the morning of Wednesday, March 23, 1911, the ship encountered a severe electrical storm. Just as the skies were clearing, a lightning bolt struck the ship's foremast, which was splintered into pieces that came crashing down to the decks below, smashing skylights and narrowly avoiding the bridge, where First Officer Charles Lightoller and others were standing.[26]

Lightoller would soon be facing a storm of another kind on board his next assignment – the RMS *Titanic*.

In December 1910, a newspaper report stated that Captain Haddock would be joining *Titanic* as well – as her commander. As it was reported in *The New York Tribune*:[27]

GET GIANTS OF THE SEA

Captains Smith and Haddock for *Olympic* and *Titanic*

Captain Herbert J. Haddock of the White Star liner *Oceanic*, which left port on Wednesday for Southampton, was congratulated by wireless yesterday on his appointment to the command of the new White Star giant steamship *Titanic*.

The news of his selection to command the biggest ship in the world and the appointment of Captain "Ted" [sic] Smith, of the *Adriatic*, to the command of the *Olympic* was brought to port yesterday by the *Majestic*.

Since the launching of the 45,000-ton *Olympic* several weeks ago at Belfast, there has been considerable speculation as to who would command her and her sister ship, the *Titanic*. There have been many candidates for the command, as the promotion from one ship to another of bigger tonnage carries with it a substantial increase in pay.

Captain Smith, who will take the *Olympic*, is the commodore of the White Star fleet. He was assigned to the *Adriatic* when she made her maiden trip to this country, his place on the *Oceanic* being taken by Captain Haddock.

Captains Haddock and Smith shared one more common experience before they would take their respective commands on *Olympic* and *Titanic*.

Captain Smith was bringing the *Olympic* over from New York when, on February 24, 1912, the ship struck a submerged wreck and dropped a blade on her port propeller. The ship was able to complete the voyage without difficulty, but she was forced to return to Harland & Wolff for repairs, thus delaying work on *Titanic*.

Just five days later, in an echo of the *Olympic*'s experience, *Oceanic* lost a propeller blade on February 29 as Haddock was bringing her over to New York. She was a day late in arriving on what would be Haddock's last westbound crossing as *Oceanic*'s skipper. Upon her return home, he would report to Belfast for his new assignment – supervising the *Titanic* until Captain Smith completed one more *Olympic* crossing.

CHAPTER 5

'*Olympic* is a marvel!'

Her sinking would make *Titanic* the most famous vessel since Noah's Ark. The story of her last night afloat captured the imagination of the world – and kept it – for generations, leaving her sister ship *Olympic* a mere footnote to history.

This is ironic considering *Titanic* never completed a single crossing while *Olympic* enjoyed a long and illustrious career spanning three decades.

Before *Titanic* arrived on the scene, however, it was *Olympic* that made the headlines:

NEW OCEAN LINER STARTS ON MAIDEN TRIP

The *Olympic*, one of the White Star Liners, Will Attempt to Break Speed Record

Southampton, England, June 14 – Enthusiastic crowds assembled about the new dock and cheered wildly as the monster White Star Liner *Olympic*, the largest and finest vessel in the world, steamed away in her maiden voyage to New York. The giant ship will attempt to make a record-breaking trip across the Atlantic.[1]

Captain E. J. Smith, whose last command had been the 729-foot, 24,000 gross ton *Adriatic*, was on *Olympic*'s bridge, ready for his newest command, which would be his last before retiring, according to a report published the week before in *The New York Times*:[2]

CHANGE IN COMMODORES

Capt. Haddock to Head White Star Line at Increased Pay

Capt. E. J. Smith, R. N. R., the Commodore of the White Star Line, who is to command the new mammoth liner *Olympic*, will retire at the end of the present year, it is understood, as he will have reached the age limit. He will be relieved by Capt. H. J. Haddock of the *Oceanic*, a naval reserve commander, the only skipper in the Atlantic trade who wears the mid-Victorian mutton chop whiskers without a beard or mustache.

She was making headlines, even if the stories were inaccurate. *Olympic* was not built for speed and had no chance of setting a speed record, and, of course, *Olympic*'s maiden voyage would not be Smith's last.

A coal strike threatened *Olympic*'s maiden voyage, just as it would for *Titanic* a year later. That was overcome through careful advanced planning in the acquisition of coal. Another threat, which emerged just before sailing day, involved crew compensation.

The day before departure, several men refused to join *Olympic*'s crew unless the White Star Line agreed to a pay increase equal to that earned by the crew of the *Lusitania* and *Mauretania*. White Star agreed to the pay increase on the morning *Olympic* sailed.[3]

J. Bruce Ismay and his wife, Florence, were aboard for the maiden voyage. Ismay was keen to thoroughly inspect the new ship and to hear what his fellow passengers thought of *Olympic* so that any improvements could be incorporated into the *Titanic*.

Also on board was the chief designer, Thomas Andrews, who was leading a guarantee group from Harland & Wolff to make sure everything was ship-shape during the voyage.

As stewardess Violet Jessop recalled:

The *Olympic* had been designed by one of the finest and kindliest of men it has been my privilege to meet: Tommy Andrews, designer for Harland & Wolff, the Belfast shipbuilder, was loved and respected throughout the fleet by everyone from the lowest scullion to the 'old man' as a real gentleman.

Perhaps we felt proprietary about this last ship because, in our small way, we were responsible for many changes and improvements. These were things of seemingly small importance to the disinterested but of tremendous help to us, improvements that would make our life aboard less arduous and make her more of a home than we had hitherto known at sea.[4]

The New York Times covered the maiden departure, noting that 'Great crowds witnessed the departure of the new craft and gave her a rousing sendoff. She carried 450 saloon passengers, a record for a westward voyage in June.'[5]

As the ship was still in mid-ocean, the *Times* offered readers a detailed description of the new liner that soon would be arriving in New York Harbor.[6]

Under the headline 'THE *OLYMPIC* LIKE A CITY', the paper described each deck of the ship and the delights to be found there, from the promenade deck, where 'are situated all of the public rooms, apart from the dining saloon and restaurant' to the bridge deck, which 'is mostly occupied by passenger accommodations, including several suites with sitting room, one or two bedrooms, and bathroom, though at its after end there is an a la carte restaurant for first class passengers and a second class smoking room.'

On board ship, passengers marveled at her size, which they had been reading about for some time. What surprised them most was her steadiness – even at higher speeds.

Bruce Ismay inspected the ship thoroughly in search of things that could be made better not only on *Olympic*, but also for her future sister ship. His observations were those of a discriminating passenger: the mattresses in first class were too springy and therefore allowed for too much motion, even on a steady ship, and the first class bathrooms lacked cigar holders.

The biggest change he requested was to enclose the forward A-Deck promenade on *Titanic* so her passengers wouldn't have to endure ocean spray as *Olympic*'s passengers had to do. The change, a fairly major one to be done so late in *Titanic*'s fitting out, would give observers an easy way to tell the sister ships apart.

Another Ismay recommendation – that some of the deck space, which he considered excessive, could be used to create additional first class staterooms – was a larger undertaking that would be incorporated into *Titanic*, then being fitted out at Harland & Wolff.

Those suggestions aside, Ismay was excited about the performance of the new ship, as he expressed in a message sent from the ship to Lord Pirrie, who didn't make the maiden trip: '*Olympic* is a marvel and has given unbounded satisfaction.'

Olympic's crew were still finding their way in the huge new liner when she approached Ambrose Channel. Stewardess Violet Jessop said:

> Hardly had we got our bearings about the ship when we had to brace ourselves for arrival in New York. Any docking day is nerve-wracking apart from the work, with the sheer enthusiasm expended everywhere. We knew the excitement would be unprecedented and that our early morning arrival off quarantine would be more hectic than usual.
>
> We were not mistaken. Bells rang from a very early hour. Strident and excited voices demanded food, for everybody aimed to be ready to great their friends with an air of complete assurance as if to impress them that this successful maiden voyage crossing was partly their personal achievement; we mere slaves obeyed instantly to assist them in the illusion. I've so often watched travelers assume that attitude.[7]

Olympic had arrived! She left Quarantine at 7:45 a.m. on the morning of June 21 and steamed up New York harbor, where her maiden appearance was greeted with appropriate fanfare.

The Trenton Evening Times noted the enthusiastic welcome and the pride of Captain Smith as his new command came steaming into harbor:

> With everything that could make a noise, making that noise with a will, the White Star liner *Olympic*, largest of the ocean greyhounds, came up the river yesterday on her maiden trip, having sailed from Southampton, with calls at Cherbourg and Queenstown. Such a greeting she got! And such a seraphic smile as her commander wore! If any person on earth was prouder than he, that person's identity hasn't been made known. His was the smile that couldn't come off.[8]

The pilot, Julius Adler, was also smiling, and seemed almost as proud of the ship as was the captain.

"She handles like a catboat," he said, comparing White Star's new flagship with a single-masted sailboat. But *Olympic* was no catboat, as she demonstrated during the hour-long docking procedure when she drew the tug *O. L. Hallenbeck* into her side, causing severe damage to the smaller vessel's stern.

Lavish publicity came in from all corners for the pride of the White Star Line, which was pulling out all the stops to generate interest in its newest vessel.

'On the second night [in New York harbor] a dinner was given to 600 White Star agents from all over the United States,' recalled stewardess Violet Jessop. 'Men of every size and age appeared, preparing to enjoy wholeheartedly the lavish hospitality White Star was offering them. Tours – much drinking – and it took many hours to reunite coats, hats and shoes with their rightful owners but everyone voted the *Olympic* and its crew "swell."'[9]

With such a party, White Star was putting an additional strain on the workers responsible for the turnaround, which would prove daunting on so large a ship, but *Olympic* was ready to sail in time for her return voyage, for which she departed on Wednesday, June 28.

Thousands of New Yorkers stood pier-side to witness the maiden departure of the biggest ship in the world, carrying nearly double the complement of passengers she had brought over on the first crossing.

Waiting for her as she departed was aviator Tom Sopwith, who had been planning a special aerial greeting for the new steamer that included dropping a parcel onto her deck. As *The New York Times* reported:

The aviator skirted the shore till his craft was over Fort Hamilton. Then he shot out over the water, still maintaining his altitude, and crossed directly over the big steamer. The big boat paid no attention, steaming majestically on. But the biplane turned to cross her again, and then from the whistles of the liner and three siren shrieks of greeting and from the whistles of every craft in the harbor went up the discordant scream, which passes for a welcome among seaman. It was then that Sopwith dropped his letter, though none on shore or on the craft seem to have seen them land.

Sopwith told reporters his parcel also contained a pair of eyeglasses that had been forgotten by a passenger on board *Olympic*, but it was later suggested that perhaps the flyover was a publicity stunt.

As the aviator related after the flight: 'We were about 1,000 feet up. Perhaps I should say just under 1,000 feet. I could feel the warm air rising from the funnels of the liner, and it bothered me just a bit - not enough to cause me real concern, however. We dropped a bundle of letters - letters for folks on board and for folks in England, but I guess they went in the water.'[10]

She reached Southampton on July 5, completing her first round-trip to America. On the next departure, J. P. Morgan would be on board to experience IMM's new wonder for himself. Lord Pirrie also joined her. Perhaps the greatest compliment paid the new ship came from a passenger on this crossing who commented, 'It is the only steamer where the chairs are not fastened to the floor, as no wave is big enough to rock it.'[11]

When *Olympic* reached New York, newspaper photographers took pictures of Captain Smith and Lord Pirrie posing proudly on her deck. The *Des Moines News* ran the photo with a headline: 'Man Who Made and Man Who Runs Biggest Steamship in the World'. The caption noted that 'Pirrie built the ship; Smith is its captain. They spent much time together on the trip across, watching the workings of the giant vessel, for Pirrie is building a sister ship, the *Titanic*, and wishes to improve, if possible, upon the *Olympic*.'[12]

Pirrie was surely pleased: the new *Olympic* class was proving popular and profitable. The proof was in the headlines. On July 26, two days before *Olympic* next departed New York, there was news of a second sister ship for the *Olympic*:[13]

NEW VESSEL WILL BE BUILT BY WHITE STAR AS SISTER SHIP OF *OLYMPIC*

New York, July 24 – After the arrival of the steamship *Baltic*, of the White Star Line, today, it was reported unofficially that the company had in view the building of a new vessel as a sister craft to the *Titanic* and the *Olympic*.

It is said that the new boat will probably be called the *Gigantic*, and when she is built her designers will correct any shortcomings that may be found in the *Olympic* or the *Titanic*.

It was said that the new steamship would be launched in 1913.

When *Olympic* next returned to New York, Captain Smith was the guest of honor at a small dinner party hosted at the Waldorf-Astoria hotel by Gen. Charles Miller and his wife. "There were large and small ships in the decorations and ices were served from a miniature *Olympic*."[14]

The good news continued. When she departed Southampton on August 30, *Olympic* carried a record number (700) of first class passengers.[15]

Journalists' preoccupation with the comings and goings of IMM's J. P. Morgan bordered on the obsessive, and *The New York Times* made space to report on Morgan's sudden appearance at *Olympic*'s New York pier just as the ship was preparing for departure on Saturday, September 9:[16]

When the *Olympic* sailed from this port Saturday J. Pierpont Morgan was at the pier to see his wife and son start on their voyage across. The financier arrived just before the hour set for sailing and rushed here and there among the crowd looking for wife and son, but failed to find them. When he dashed up the gangplank the all ashore gong was then being sounded. He soon descended it again. As he reached the pier he spied Mrs. Morgan elbowing to a place at the rail. Mr. Morgan ran back on board, gave his wife a kiss and reached the pier just as the order was given to lower the gangplank.

On September 18, 1911, White Star issued its 1911/12 sailing schedule, which for the first time announced that *Titanic* would depart on her maiden voyage on March 20, 1912.

Olympic was poised to carry a record number of passengers across the Atlantic with her return crossing from Southampton on September 20, 1911. The majority of first cabin passengers were Americans returning from the end of the season in Europe.[18]

The timing of the *Titanic* announcement and *Olympic*'s would-be accomplishment was unfortunate, however, given that events would force the cancellation of *Olympic*'s voyage and a rescheduling of *Titanic*'s debut.

Olympic departed Southampton for the fifth time just after 11 a.m. on September 20. A heavy haze hung over the water, but the weather was otherwise clear and the ship was able to navigate a course up the Cowes roadstead north of the Isle of Wight under the guidance of Southampton pilot George Bowyer.

Olympic had just completed a series of turns to clear the Bramble shoal and was accelerating when the 7,770 ton, 360 foot British cruiser *Hawke* came alongside on a parallel course. Captain Smith, also on the bridge, watched *Hawke* begin to fall behind *Olympic*.

As he would later testify in court, *Hawke*'s captain ordered his ship 'hard a port' and repeated the order when, inexplicably, his ship turned the wrong way, toward the *Olympic*'s side.

Captain Smith told Bowyer, 'I don't believe he will get under our stern, Bowyer.' The pilot asked if the two ships were going to hit, and Captain Smith replied, 'Yes! He is starboarding and he is going to hit us. She's going to strike us in the stern.'

Bowyer had only begun to turn *Olympic*'s wheel when *Hawke*'s steel-reinforced bow, which had been designed to ram and sink enemy ships, cut into the *Olympic*'s stern on the starboard side like a knife through butter.

The sound of the collision was deafening, and the two ships reeled under the force of it. *Hawke* developed a perceptible list and only quick work with collision mats and pumps saved the naval craft.

Outwardly, *Olympic* seemed to withstand the collision with little trouble. However, the damage was extensive, including an eight-foot V-shaped gouge along the stern and a larger, more serious gash below the waterline that flooded two compartments completely and partially filled a third.

Steerage passengers had gone to lunch. Otherwise, as papers noted in their coverage, the accident could have had human casualties:

> The hole thus caused was much larger than the upper rent, and had it been night, with the people asleep in their berths when the collision occurred, a more melancholy story might have been told.

One second class passenger, a Dr Downton of Pennsylvania, narrowly escaped being one such casualty. 'I was lying on a couch in the berth, reading a book, only a few seconds before the collision occurred,' he said, 'when my friend looked in the door, and said, "Come along for you will be late for luncheon." I got up and went out, and immediately afterwards the cruiser had carried away that part of the berth where I was lying.'

A portion of Downton's cabin, and a bag carrying items worth £80, fell into the sea when *Hawke*'s bow withdrew from the gash. The bag was later retrieved from the sea and turned over to Customs officials at Cowes, where Downton retrieved it.

A passenger watching over her baby in a cabin just down the hall from Downton's described the noise of the collision as terrifying. First, there was the sound of the iron plates being rended, followed by the breaking off of rivets and the surge of rushing water. Smoke filled the halls to such an extent that she thought the ship might even be on fire.

Within the hour White Star was informed of the collision by wireless from *Olympic* herself. Captain Smith reported that *Olympic*'s compartments flooded so rapidly that he ran her ashore but that the watertight bulkheads were holding. The ship's passengers were lining her rails and the lifeboats were ready for lowering. There was no danger, he related, of loss of life.

The news was most unwelcome, coming as it did when *Olympic* was carrying her record number (732 first class, 497 second class and 874 third class) of passengers for the westward crossing. Among the more illustrious passengers were Waldorf Astor; New York Central Railroad President W. C. Brown and his wife; and American Ambassador to Tokyo Charles Page Bryan. Also on board was a passenger who would be aboard *Titanic* next April – Harry Widener.

Indian prince Jaisingh Gaekwar, whose father was the Gaekwar of Baroda, was sailing back to America to return to his studies at Harvard. He told reporters that there was no panic on board ship, but that everyone seemed to be 'more disgusted than frightened' because of the difficulty they would have in finding passage to New York as this was the end of the winter season in Europe.

Indeed, the gong that announced luncheon was rung in First Class just ten minutes after the collision, and as Edgar B. Davies of the General Rubber Company of New York would later state, nearly every one left the upper deck and went inside for the meal.

After inspecting the damaged portions of his ship along with the chief officer, Captain Smith decided it was safe to return his ship to port under her own steam. Tugs arrived to assist both ships, and by 4 p.m. *Olympic* was listing to starboard as a result of her injuries.

Captain Smith reported to his passengers that the voyage would have to be cancelled and the ship returned to port for repairs. A few passengers returned to Southampton by tug that night, including Harry Widener, while the bulk of her passengers and crew remained on board for the night as the ship remained at anchor at Osborne Bay.

One impatient passenger – Thomas Magee of San Francisco – took matters into his own hands. Realizing the *Olympic* would not be proceeding to America, Magee decided he had to find a way back to shore to secure passage on another ship so that he and his wife could get back to the children they had waiting for them at home.[18]

I was looking out of a port just after it all happened and saw right below a butcher's boy who had rowed out from shore in a dandy little boat. "There's two pounds if you put me ashore," I called to him, and he signaled "right".

There was just room for me to squeeze through that port, and I made fast a rope and loosed it. But that rope scarcely reached half way to the water, and I had to pull it up and fix another to it. All the time I feared that some of the ship's officers would see me and stop it, for I was dead keen to get those passages, knowing what a rush there would be later.

Down the rope I went, a good fifty feet of it, and hung there at the end. There was a tidy sea running, and my lad could not get his boat near me for a bit and I must have dangled like that for quite five minutes before the boat was below me and I dropped into it.

Once Magee and the little boat reached Cowes, he called White Star's Southampton office and booked three of the seven remaining berths on *Adriatic*, which was due to depart Liverpool the next day.

Assisted by tugs, *Olympic* returned to her Southampton dock at 11 a.m. the next day. Newspapers on both sides of the Atlantic were filled with reports on the collision – and in imagery that foreshadowed the larger disaster to come, Captain Smith and his crippled ship illustrated story after story:[19]

> How quickly gaiety and pleasant anticipation can be turned into gloom and disappointment was pathetically revealed to-day as the mighty *Olympic*, with two gaping wounds in her starboard side, the result of the collision with the cruiser *Hawke*, lay in the new dock. No lives had been lost, but there was misery among groups of third-class passengers as box after box of luggage, saturated with water, was brought ashore from the hold that had been swamped owing to the liner being rammed.

Among the distraught third-class passengers were three English brides-to-be, bound for America and their waiting grooms, whose wedding dresses were brought ashore in trunks saturated by sea water.[20]

> Two of the young women were particularly grieved, not only by the loss of their bridal dresses, but because of the delay in sailing. The third was a little less emotional. "He's waited for me for five years; I think he will wait a little longer."
>
> There were few whose baggage had not been spoilt or damaged by water in the hold, and it was pathetic to watch the third-class passengers as they watched their large 'not wanted' trunks brought from the hold.

Another *Olympic* passenger, an elderly woman, bemoaned the loss of a bag full of items she'd obtained during four months spent visiting relatives in England. 'I suppose it is partly my own fault,' she said. 'We came second-class, and my husband wanted to return by the same class on the *Cedric*. But the *Olympic* being a new boat, I thought it would be so nice to return in her, even if we could only get third class accommodation. And here we are.'

Other steamship lines were called into action to assist in expediting *Olympic's* record number of passengers to their destinations as quickly as possible. Due to the large number of people involved, all ten steamship lines that sailed on Sunday, September 24 carried refugees of the *Olympic*.[21]

A rush for the *Mauretania's* Saturday sailing left many disappointed, as the Cunarder had room for only thirty passengers in first class. Harry Widener was one of the lucky few who secured passage on board, and he returned on the vessel along with his uncle, Joseph Widener.

With the *Olympic* back in Ocean Dock, divers were able to get the first look at the underwater damage, which was discovered to be quite extensive. Aside from the two visible wounds in her side, *Olympic* had also suffered damage to her starboard propeller, with each blade having been chipped by contact with the warship.

Temporary repairs were made to the ship – with wood and steel being used to seal the damage above and below the water line.

On October 4, the ship sailed for Belfast, where she would undergo extensive repairs. *Olympic* arrived at Harland & Wolff the next day, where she found that her sister, *Titanic*, had been moved aside so that repairs could be made.[22]

The *Hawke* collision had come as a nasty surprise to White Star. The line had already faced the humiliation of cancelling its biggest sailing yet – and at the height of the post-winter exodus from Europe. Forced to rely on rival lines to accommodate the customers, White Star was further burdened by the loss of income while *Olympic* was undergoing repairs. All told, she would miss three round trips before returning to service.

Furthermore, work on the *Titanic* was put on hold in order repair *Olympic* as quickly as possible, which now put immense pressure on the shipyard – and the line – to get *Titanic* ready to sail on her maiden voyage, which had now been changed to April 10, 1912.

Finally, White Star found itself embroiled in ongoing litigation to resolve which ship – *Olympic* or *Hawke* – was to blame for the collision. The Admiralty division laid final blame on the *Olympic*, whose pilot failed to establish that the *Hawke* was in fact an overtaking vessel and for failing to give the *Hawke* adequate right of way.

As it turned out, the case would outlive the *Titanic* and reached the House of Lords in 1914, which dismissed the case while upholding the findings of the Admiralty division.

Perhaps the most disturbing result of the *Hawke* collision, however, was the effect it seemed to have on public opinion. Far from casting doubt on the safety of so large a ship, the *Hawke* collision seemed to solidify the public's faith in the ship's invincibility.

It appeared that the ship had survived the worst-case scenario – a collision that compromised two or more of her watertight compartments. Not only that – she'd been struck by a warship whose nose was specifically designed to sink enemy ships. Yet *Olympic*'s watertight compartments had performed exactly as promised – and the ship had been able to return to port under her own steam.

A statement made by Captain Smith in early 1912 and included in coverage of the on-going *Olympic-Hawke* litigation left little doubt where he stood on the issue.

Anyhow, the *Olympic* is unsinkable, and the *Titanic* will be the same when she is put in commission. Why, either of these vessels could be cut in halves and each half would remain afloat indefinitely. The non-sinkable vessel has been reached in these two wonderful craft. I venture to add that even if the engines and boilers of these vessels were to fall through their bottoms the vessels would remain afloat.

Olympic had been out of service more than two months when, on November 30, 1911, she departed Southampton for the first time since the *Hawke* collision. She was carrying 1,200 passengers.[23]

New York City gave the ship a hearty welcome when she arrived on December 7.[24]

> Welcomed by shrill blasts from many tugboats and the hoarse salutes of the ferryboat foghorns, the White Star liner *Olympic* moved slowly up the harbor to her pier yesterday after an absence of nearly three months caused by her collision with the British cruiser *Hawke* in the Solent.

The voyage had not been smooth sailing. Rough seas sent giant waves rolling across the forward decks, smashing ventilators and breaking three portholes in third class.

Professional gamblers, a common problem on ocean liners of the day, were on board in two groups for this crossing. The smoking room steward intervened when it developed that one passenger lost $1,000 to the professional gamblers.

For the first time in her career, *Olympic* was turned around for a return voyage in just two days. There was 'a good deal of hustling to get her cleaned, stored and coaled' in time.

> Fourteen gangs of coalies have worked day and night to put 6,000 tons of coal into the ship to get it all finished early this morning so that the sailors could wash decks and clean ship before the passengers came aboard. The *Olympic* consumes on an average 670 tons of coal each twenty-four hours, which is considered very economical for her size and speed. The *Lusitania* and *Mauretania* average about 1,050 each for twenty-four hours.[25]

The challenge of meeting such a tight deadline was made worse by an unexpected visit:

> Her 720 cabin passengers had not left the ship two hours on Thursday when notice came from the White Star office that 1,080 members of the American Engineers' Society would visit the *Olympic* at 2 p.m. What Purser McElroy, known familiarly as "the Eastern Despot," and Chief Steward Latimer said when they heard this news was improper, and what Chief Engineer Fleming, who had got all his staff busy below overhauling gear, said was unthinkable.
>
> When the leading members of the engineers' party went to Mr. Fleming's cabin later in the afternoon to see about going below he asked them if they were all furnished with special permits to see the engine room, as required by the White Star regulations.
>
> Opening a blue book on his desk, Mr. Fleming pointed out the regulation.
>
> "There you are," said Mr. Fleming pointing out the regulation. "You must wait until the *Olympic* is in port another trip and come down, all of you, with the special permits. Don't wait until the ship has been in dock for three or four hours, but be waiting for the gangway to be run out."

Olympic was one day out of New York when the world ushered in the new year: 1912. When the ship reached Southampton on January 5, her passengers were surprised to learn that the rather reclusive – or at least elusive – J. P. Morgan had been aboard for the crossing.[26]

On January 8, White Star announced a change in scheduling for the *Olympic* that would relieve the strain of rapid turnarounds.

Commencing with her next arrival in port, on Jan. 17, the White Star Liner *Olympic* will have a week in port each trip until March, instead of turning round in three days, as she has been doing so far. This will give the officers and crew a chance to rest and overhaul the ship thoroughly, and will relieve the strain on the liner. Last voyage the *Olympic* arrived on a Thursday morning and sailed at noon on Saturday.[27]

Olympic again encountered rough seas on the voyage that ended January 17.

Last Sunday an enormous sea curled over the bows, lifted the big forward hatch, weighing 4 tons, about 10 feet above deck, and carried it against a ventilator, which it demolished. The hatch then fell into the well forming the foredeck.[28]

On her next voyage, *Olympic* found herself the vessel of choice when American multi-millionaire John Jacob Astor made a hasty exit from New York early in 1912.

Astor, whose family had amassed one of the largest fortunes in America through the fur trade and real estate investments in New York and beyond, had divorced his first wife, the former Ava Willing of Philadelphia, in the fall of 1909. The scandal of the divorce was particularly intense given the Astors' long-standing place among New York society, but the shock was eclipsed by Astor's re-marriage a short time later.

On September 9, 1911, the forty-seven-year-old Astor married eighteen-year-old Madeleine Talmadge Force at a private ceremony at Beechwood, his Newport, Rhode Island estate. The nuptials had been condemned by the Episcopal Church, led by the Revd George Chalmers Richmond. In his sermon of August 6, 1911, which was called 'The Coming Astor Wedding and What the Episcopal Church Thinks About It,' Richmond proclaimed:[29]

The Episcopal Church is opposed to divorce. We scorn unholy alliances, both among the poor of our slums, and the rich society dwellers of Newport, Bar Harbor and other sinners' summer retreats. We abhor this Astor alliance. It is unholy in its origin, and its end will be a defiance of God's laws and of our holy religion.

We need a national uniform divorce law which will put an end to this overriding of court decrees by John Jacob Astor and the social freaks with whom he associates. So, today I denounce from this pulpit this coming Astor wedding. It is an outrage on common decency. It arouses all our moral anger.

The Episcopal Church is opposed to this alliance. It is contrary to our canons, and Mr. Astor will be socially ostracized by the best people, the minute he contracts the bargain already made.

Astor had been forbidden from marrying in New York City by the conditions of his divorce agreement, and in the end he had to pay a minister $1,000 to perform the ceremony.[30]

Word of the Astor nuptials brought a new wave of bad press, and the couple was nearly universally condemned among New York society and in newspapers across the country, as illustrated by this editorial:[31]

FOR SALE – A WOMAN

Marriage for love is looked upon by the American public as one of the noblest of things, and divorce is viewed somewhat as a matter of course; but the sale of a good woman to a man is looked upon with aversion and disgust. Had Col Astor wooed and won Miss Madeline Force for herself alone, and had the woman accepted him for his value as a man, says the *Danville Commercial News*, the world would have looked on and smiled and perhaps applauded the wedding of May and December, but as Astor had virtually bought his bride the world is disgusted and is frankly saying so ...

In this country marriages are supposed to be contracted for love, and a great majority of them are, but Col. Astor is making a settlement of millions on Miss Force leads the people to believe the little god Cupid has had nothing to do with the match. More the shame.

There can be no love in such an alliance, and it will very likely end as unhappily as Col Astor's previous venture. It is bad enough for this man, who is old enough to be the grandfather of the bride-elect, to wed this young girl; but it is nauseating for the girl to put a price on herself, and no credit to Astor to pay it. Buying women is a relic of other days, and will never become a common custom in this country, because the fathers and mothers of young women are not avaricious enough to sanction such marriages.

From one section of this country to the other Astor is being condemned for marrying this young girl so soon after his divorce, and perhaps deservedly so; but he is certainly deserving of censure and condemnation for buying the girl as though she were a chattel. As for Miss Force, well, perhaps she is too young and thoughtless to realize that she is bringing the solemn sacrament of marriage down to the low level of legalized prostitution. She is to be pitied more than blamed.

The Astors endured months of such vitriol. Col. Astor had planned a dinner party for the evening of January 22 at his famous mansion at 840 Fifth Avenue in the hopes that New York society would warm to his young bride. The invitations went out two months early, but the snubs and snipes continued unabated, and Astor cancelled the fete a week before it was to have taken place, announcing instead his intention to sail for Europe with the new Mrs Astor.[32]

The couple boarded the *Olympic* at her New York pier on sailing day – Thursday, January 25, 1912.[33] 'Mrs. Astor was a picture of health yesterday and Colonel Astor walked up the gangplank as sprightly as a youth.'

A reporter who found Astor 'alone near his suite on the sun deck' asked him about the cancelled dinner party and got an earful from the multi-millionaire about New York society.

The Colonel, as if to fire a parting shot in that with which he had had some mysterious falling out, replied warmly.

"My boy, don't ask me what I think of New York society, because it would pain me to tell you my exact feelings. I am thoroughly disgusted with it, at any rate. In fact, it is rotten, very rotten. I don't care what New York society is doing, what it has done or what it is going to do. I am disgusted with it. I am going to Egypt and I may never return."

Olympic sailed with the Astor party, accompanied by Margaret Brown of Denver, on January 24.

The ship enjoyed uneventful crossings until the following month, when on Saturday, February 24 she struck a submerged wreck in mid-ocean and lost a propeller blade. Whitelaw Reid, Ambassador to the Court of St James, was on board during the incident. He had been confined to his cabin with a cold for the duration of the trip.[34]

A reporter on board filed stories about the mishap from the ship via wireless:

Previous to the accident the vessel had beaten her record for speed, going at an average of 23 knots per hour, but the breaking of the propeller of course caused her to slow down. The accident was accompanied by a considerable shock, but there was no other damage than that to the propeller, and the passengers were perfectly calm. The ship will go to drydock for repairs.

When the accident occurred the nearest land was 750 miles west of us, but in spite of this, by means of wireless telegraphy, it was possible to send the mishap direct to Cape Race, Newfoundland. The two operators on the *Olympic* are E. J. Moore and A. Bagot.

Olympic was able to reach land under her own steam but was forced to return to Harland & Wolff for repairs, once again causing delays in the completion of *Titanic*, which was scheduled for an April 10 maiden voyage.

Olympic returned to service on March 13, when she next departed Southampton for New York. Upon her arrival, passenger, Dr A. P. L. Pease, known in his Ohio hometown as 'the globetrotter of Massilon,' regaled his fellow Massilonians with his descriptions of the White Star liner.[35]

Dr Pease's room was carpeted all over with a velvet carpet and contained a single bed, clothespress with full length mirror and drawers, stationary washstand with hot and cold water, a dressing case, a large sofa, two book shelves, electric lights, an easy chair and an electric stove. He said that the dining room would seat 260 and was equipped with sideboards sixteen feet wide carved from white oak. Electric fire places were in all of the lounging rooms.

"It is the finest ship I ever saw," said Dr Pease, "and it would pay any one interested in ship building to go to New York to see it."

CHAPTER 6
'We've Lost Touch'

Ships that had heard *Titanic*'s distress signals continued – in vain – to contact the ship, but none made its intentions more clear than *Olympic*, which signaled the wireless station at Cape Race several times: 'Going to assistance of *Titanic*.' By 2.30 a.m., she was going, indeed – faster than she'd ever gone before.

Captain Haddock had ordered every ounce of steam put to *Olympic*'s engines. It had taken some time for the ship to respond, but she had now surpassed her cruising speed of 18 ½ knots and was steaming full ahead at 23 to 24 knots per hour. The ship's rhythm was stronger than ever.

As *Olympic*'s passengers slept, the ship's crew continued to prepare for the rescue operation that would transfer passengers and crew from the *Titanic*. The work was done as quietly as possible. Captain Haddock made it clear he didn't want word of *Titanic*'s accident spreading beyond those who needed to know.

Titanic had asked *Olympic* to have her lifeboats ready, and on Captain Haddock's orders, sailors were now doing just that – removing the covers from *Olympic*'s sixteen wooden lifeboats and swinging them out on their davits.

Nobody knew what lay ahead – but *Olympic* and her crew intended to be ready.

There had been no further communication from *Titanic*. Despite on-going efforts to connect with *Titanic* or get news of her from other ships, the wireless operators' response was unchanging: 'We've lost touch.'[1]

With all that *Olympic* had learned in the past few hours –the increased desperation of *Titanic*'s cries for help, the talk of lifeboats being lowered and an engine room flooding, a message that was cut off abruptly, followed by wireless silence – it would have seemed reasonable to assume that *Titanic* was gone.

It was also possible to believe the stricken liner had lost power and was out there, damaged but afloat, awaiting rescue.

Even now, there seemed reason to hope that the unsinkable *Titanic* would survive what was apparently a serious collision. Recent experience, in fact, had conditioned sea captains and their crews – not to mention passengers – to have faith in the modern ships that plied the North Atlantic.

Only five years before, on March 17, 1907, Captain Thomas J. Jones was bringing the 12,000-ton *Suevic* on one last voyage to Plymouth before his retirement after thirty-nine years at sea. As the ship neared shore, she encountered rough seas just as she approached the hazard-filled area off the coast of Cornwall known to sailors as the Lizard.[2]

At 10.27 p.m., the lookouts saw rocks in the ship's path and shouted 'Breakers ahead!' It was too late. The ship struck rocks at her full speed of 13 knots and was grounded. With more than a third of the ship hopelessly stuck on the rocks, the ship's company was evacuated over a six-hour period.

With the most valuable two-thirds of the ship unharmed, White Star decided to use explosives to separate the undamaged section from the grounded bow. On March 26, explosive charges did just that, and the freed after portion of *Suevic* was towed to dry dock in Southampton. Meanwhile, Harland & Wolff began construction on a new bow section for the ship.

Suevic was now being called the longest ship in the world – with her stern in Southampton and her bow in Belfast.

The two parts were mated on November 4, 1907 and after two months of work, *Suevic* was back in service.

Here was another example of the invincibility of modern steamships. Even when grounded and blown in half, *Suevic* survived to steam another day.

Photos of the severed bow and the rejoined ship caught more attention in the popular press than did the findings of the Board of Trade's inquiry into the *Suevic* incident, which found that:

> The stranding of the *Suevic* was caused by continuing towards land at high speed in thick, heavy weather, without making any allowances for tide or current, and continuing the same course and speed after the light was seen without taking the usual precaution of using the lead to verify position.

The board found Captain Jones responsible for the wreck and suspended his Master's Certificate for three months, a rather hollow gesture given that his retirement was by then in effect.

Another White Star calamity two years later also served to reinforce the public's faith in the modern class of ocean liners.

The White Star liner *Republic*, a 570-foot, 15,000 ton single-funneled twin-screw steamer, collided with the Lloyd Italiano line's SS *Florida* on January 23, 1909 while steaming through a dense fog off the coast of Nantucket, Massachusetts.

The *Florida*'s bow was crushed, and the *Republic* was struck amidships, where her engine room and boiler rooms began to take on water. While Captain Inman Sealby mustered the passengers and kept them calm, *Republic*'s wireless operator, Jack Binns, sent the new distress signal CQD. Soon several ships, including the Coast Guard cutter *Gresham* and White Star's own *Baltic*, were alongside the *Republic*, which had developed a pronounced list.

The force of the collision had collapsed three of the wireless cabin's four walls, but Binns had remained at his post.[3]

> The ship was filling fast and Binns, realizing that all hope of bringing help lay in his messages, went to a storeroom in search of storage batteries or concentrators. He had to dive into a water-filled compartment and swim and wade around until he found the batteries.
>
> He then rigged his instrument with these batteries, and in less than half an hour after his instrument had been silenced feeble waves were once more spurting forth

into the fog-filled air beseeching all within hearing to hasten the rescue of the *Republic*.

All but six people were rescued from the *Republic*, which remained afloat for nearly 40 hours before she finally sank. While ultimately the ship was lost, the focus of the world was on the miraculous wireless apparatus and the wireless operators, including *Baltic*'s Henry J. Tattersall, who had brough rescue for nearly all on board *Republic*.[4]

> That was a great achievement of wireless telegraphy, in saving the lives of more than sixteen hundred passengers from the steamers *Republic* and *Florida* which collided off Nantucket early Saturday morning. The brief messages exchanged by the operators are as thrilling as a novel, and Operator Tattersall, who remained constantly at his key without sleep for fifty-two hours, is a hero. Wireless telegraphy has become an important factor in navigation, and some seamen believe that if the *Florida* had been equipped with instruments the collision could not have happened.

When *Republic*'s operator, Jack Binns, reached New York he was given a hero's welcome, including a ticker tape parade. He became a household name and was the subject of a song, a short film and a play called *Via Wireless*.

Binns returned to service for White Star on the *Adriatic* under the command of E. J. Smith. Ironically, it was his notoriety that kept Binns from being transferred to the *Olympic*. White Star officials apparently wanted to distance themselves from the *Republic* disaster. Binns left White Star and in the spring of 1912 went to work for William Randolph Hearst as a wireless operator for the *New York American*. He started work in the second week of April, just as *Titanic* was in the midst of her maiden voyage.

The *Republic* disaster confirmed what the White Star Line and other steamship companies were now claiming – that while modern ships may suffer damage, they will remain afloat long enough for wireless calls to attract help from nearby ships.

Olympic herself was victim of an accident that, rather than pointing to the dangers of ocean travel, underscored the public's enduring faith in steamships of the day and seemed to confirm, just months before *Titanic* sank, that the *Olympic*-class liners were indeed unsinkable.

CHAPTER 7

'More Serious News Might Come Later'

International Mercantile Marine Vice President Philip Franklin was asleep at his home on New York's Upper East Side when the phone rang shortly after 2 a.m. local time on the morning of April 15. On the line was Charles E. Crane of the Associated Press.[1]

Crane informed Franklin that the news agency was getting reports that the *Titanic* was sinking and had sent a call for assistance. Franklin asked for the source of the information and was told it came from the liner *Virginian* via Montreal.

The first report had indeed come from Canada, where an Allan Line employee told a Montreal reporter that *Titanic* had asked the *Virginian* for help after having struck an iceberg. The *Montreal Gazette*, which had a content-sharing arrangement with *The New York Times*, passed the information along to the *Times*, where Managing Editor Carr Van Anda was about to oversee the scoop of the century.

Franklin responded to Crane's call by bawling out the reporter, as Crane recalled: 'Stuff and nonsense it was to him. The *Titanic* would shatter an iceberg into a frappé. He hung up with: "Don't call me again with such silly information."'

Failing to secure a comment from Franklin, Crane proceeded to write a story that suggested the *Titanic* was sinking with a large loss of life.

Meanwhile, Franklin attempted to gather information on his own. He called the White Star dock, where officials relayed that they had no information but had been fielding calls from reporters. Franklin next called the Associated Press office and asked the news agency to hold off on reporting the story until it could be confirmed. He was told it was too late; the story was already out.

He had been unable to kill the story completely as initial reports had indeed already been issued to newspapers on both sides of the Atlantic. But Franklin's call did have the desired effect with respect to Crane's story. Crane was asleep at home an hour later when a call came in from the AP copy desk. The White Star Line was denying the story and Associated Press editors had decided to kill Crane's story.

Information was needed at this early hour, and Franklin now drew upon the company's considerable resources in a search to find it. He contacted the line's Montreal office in an effort to confirm the report from the *Virginian*. He next called the head of IMM's steamship department, who was instructed to contact the captain of the *Olympic*.

'I did not want to alarm the captain of the *Olympic*,' Franklin said. 'So all I asked in the telegram was, "Can you get the position of the *Titanic*? Wire us immediately her position."'

J. Bruce Ismay, chairman of the White Star Line, commissioned the construction of the *Olympic* and *Titanic* as a way to compete with the rival Cunard Line's new *Lusitania* and *Mauretania*. (Author's Collection)

ENTRANCE TO BELFAST HARBOUR.

Belfast Harbor and the Harland & Wolff shipyard as they appeared at the time of the construction of *Olympic* and *Titanic*. Photographed from a near-completed *Olympic*, *Titanic* is still on the stocks. (J & C McCutcheon Collection)

Titanic (left) and *Olympic* (right) were built side by side under the Arrol Gantry at the Harland & Wolff shipyard in Belfast. (Author's Collection)

Her enormous hull was painted a light gray to make *Olympic* stand out amid the framework of the Arrol Gantry in which she was built. (J & C McCutcheon Collection)

The stern of the *Olympic* jutting out from the Arrol Gantry at Harland & Wolff. (J & C McCutcheon Collection)

1908 was a busy year for Thomas Andrews, who married and became a father at the same time as he was overseeing the construction of *Olympic* and *Titanic*. (Author's Collection)

Launch of the Largest Vessel in the World. The White Star Liner "Olympic" at Harland & Wolff's Shipyard, Belfast

Olympic was launched on October 20, 1910. 'In accordance with the custom of the White Star Line there was no christening ceremony.' (J & C McCutcheon Collection)

Olympic was a source of pride for Belfast and the Harland & Wolff shipyard, as evidenced by this group photo of shipyard workers in front of *Olympic's* massive hull. In all, more than 15,000 men were needed to build the immense liner. (J & C McCutcheon Collection)

Olympic nearing completion. By now her funnels and lifeboats have been added. (J & C McCutcheon Collection)

With the *Olympic* nearly ready for service, the shipyard had also completed a new dry dock large enough to accommodate her and the sister ships she was meant to have in the future. (J & C McCutcheon Collection)

Olympic is floated into the world's largest graving dock – Thompson graving dock – in Belfast. (J & C McCutcheon Collection)

The pride of the White Star Line in profile, showing her clean lines and impressive size to maximum effect. (J & C McCutcheon Collection)

In late May 1911, *Olympic* was towed into Belfast Lough for the sea trials that were required by the British Board of Trade in order to certify her seaworthiness. (J & C McCutcheon Collection)

Olympic was put through her paces for the first time during two days of sea trials in late May 1911. (J & C McCutcheon Collection)

Dressed with flags from stem to stern, *Olympic* arrived in her home port of Liverpool on June 1, 1911, where she would be open for public inspection for a few hours. (J & C McCutcheon Collection)

The A La Carte Restaurant on *Olympic*. As one passenger remarked in 1911, 'It is the only steamer where the chairs are not fastened to the floor, as no wave is big enough to rock it.' (J & C McCutcheon Collection)

Olympic's first class smoking room was a men-only retreat where one could enjoy a cigar and brandy amid the lush mahogany panelled walls with stained glass windows. (Library of Congress)

Nothing epitomized *Olympic's* luxurious appointments more than her Grand Staircase. As one crew member remarked, 'I sensed at once that she was going to be a kindly ship'. (William H. Rau Collection)

Olympic's boat deck, as seen from the second class entrance (at left), provided a large area for walking or sitting on the deck. The original plan called for sixty-four lifeboats instead of the sixteen she carried in davits. (William H. Rau Collection)

HYTHE PIER. OLYMPIC PASSING.

Olympic, dwarfing all other vessels as she passes Hythe Pier. She 'looked colossal and even "uncanny" as she towered high above the waterline.' (J & C McCutcheon Collection)

Olympic dressed with flags in Southampton harbor prior to her maiden voyage. The pilot, George Bowyer, was used to ever-larger ships, but was duly impressed by *Olympic* when she first arrived in the harbor. 'We could hardly believe our eyes there was such a ship!' (J & C McCutcheon Collection)

Captain Smith was commodore of the White Star Line and the highest-paid captain in the trade when he took command of the new flagship, *Olympic*, in May 1911. The following spring he would take command of the new *Titanic* in time for her maiden voyage. He was popular with passengers and had become known as 'the millionnaire's captain'. (Author's Collection)

The White Star Line's *Majestic* was Captain Smith's first command. (J & C McCutcheon Collection)

Adriatic, another of Captain Smith's commands, leaving New York. (J & C McCutcheon Collection)

The desire to avoid panic was now epidemic, having influenced the designs this morning of Captain Smith, Captain Haddock and Philip Franklin as they struggled to maintain order in the face of disaster.

Olympic received the first inquiry from Franklin at 4.15 a.m. ship's time, which was relayed to the ship via Sable Island. It read: 'Captain Haddock *Olympic* – Endeavor communicate *Titanic* and ascertain time and position Reply as soon as possible to Ismay New York.'

Captain Haddock was now aware that the New York office was tuned in to *Titanic's* situation. He sent the following inquiry to Cape Race: 'Have you any particulars of *Titanic*?' There was no new information.

The picture from mid-Atlantic was fuzzy, but Franklin was now taking control of matters from New York. He summoned all important personnel to join him in the New York office on Broadway, and upon arriving there he was greeted with the following memo:

Titanic. Received from Associated Press from Cape Race 3.05 AM Monday, April 15. 10.25 PM EST, *Titanic* called CQD; reported having struck iceberg and required immediate assistance. Half an hour afterwards, reported that they were sinking by the head. Women were being put off in boats and weather calm and clear. Gave position as 41.46 north, 50.14 west. Stop this station. Notified Allan liner *Virginian*, who immediately advised he was proceeding toward scene of disaster. Stop. *Virginian* at midnight stated was about 170 miles distant from *Titanic* and expected reach there about 10 AM. *Olympic*, at 4.24 PM GMT in latitude 40.32 north, longitude 61.18 west, was in direct communication with *Titanic* and is now making all haste toward her. *Baltic*, at 1.15 AM EST reported himself as about 200 miles east of *Titanic*, and was also making toward her. Last signals from *Titanic* were heard by *Virginian* at 12.25 AM EST. He reported them blurred and ending abruptly.

Franklin had quickly mobilized his team to deal with the flood of inquiries from reporters. Soon, worried relatives of *Titanic* passengers would add their voices to the cacophony. By Monday morning they would be fielding inquiries by all corners of society, from the poorest immigrant all the way up to Astors, Guggenheims and the President of the United States.

Franklin, forty-one, had been named a vice president just a few months after the formation of IMM in 1902. He had previously been in charge of the business of the Atlantic Transport Line, which would become part of the IMM conglomerate. An administrator at heart, Franklin had no seafaring experience beyond that of a passenger.

For nearly 10 years, Franklin had worked closely with Bruce Ismay to ensure the smooth operation of White Star ships on the US side of things. With the arrival of the massive new *Olympic* in June 1911, Franklin and the company's US officials were faced with a new challenge. The ship was intended to be a Wednesday to Saturday ship, meaning she would arrive in New York on a Wednesday and depart the following Saturday. This allowed only three days to coal the ship and refit her with clean linens and enough food and drink for the voyage.

The schedule was a goal for the future, and one that in her first two New York departures, *Olympic* failed to achieve, leaving the following Wednesday in each case.

After *Olympic*'s second westbound crossing, Franklin first made the suggestion to Ismay that perhaps *Olympic* could be pushed to arrive in New York on Tuesday evenings. Ismay responded in a letter dated July 27, 1911:[2]

> Your strong recommendation that the *Olympic*, on her next voyage, should be allowed to dock on Tuesday evening, will receive consideration, and I note you say that she could have done this easily on her last voyage. I do not quite gather whether your recommendation goes so far as to advocate our always attempting to land passengers on Tuesday; perhaps you will let me hear from you on this.
>
> I at once admit that docking on Tuesday evening would help you in turning the ship round, and give those on board a better chance of getting the ship in good shape for the Saturday sailing, and further, that if we could make it a practice to do this, it would please the passengers, but as I have repeatedly stated, I feel very strongly that passengers would be far more satisfied to know, when they left here, that they would not land until Wednesday morning, rather than be in a state of uncertainty in regard to this for the whole of the trip. I do not think you can have ever experienced the miseries of a night landing in New York; had you done so, I think your views might be altered.

Franklin continued to press for a Tuesday evening arrival schedule for *Olympic*, to which Ismay sent another letter dated July 31, 1911:

> I am afraid, if you keep on writing me much more in regard to the *Olympic* docking in New York on Tuesday evening, I shall have to reply to you in the same manner as you did to Mr Curry when he kept finding fault with the stamp of firemen you are supplying to the American Line steamers at New York.
>
> As you are aware, I am not favourably disposed to trying to land passengers on Tuesday afternoon, but if, after talking the matter over with Lord Pirrie, Captain Smith and Mr Bell the consensus of opinion is in favour of this being done, you may rest assured I will not allow my individual feeling to stand in the way.

On August 4, 1911, the New York office sent a reply to Ismay which read:

> Mr Franklin's letter of July 20th which crossed yours under acknowledgment will have made it clear to you that his suggestion for a Tuesday evening arrival here applied generally and was not confined only to the steamer's next voyage. We shall be very interested to hear the result of your deliberations with Lord Pirrie to-day on this subject ...

Ismay eventually agreed to the Tuesday night arrival plan, although it was never realized in practice. In a letter to Captain Smith dated August 11, 1911, Ismay issued the following edict:

We confirm the verbal instructions given to you at Southampton last week that it will be right for you to go full speed when on the short track, subject to your considering it prudent and in the interests of safe navigation to do so. This instruction applies to both eastbound and westbound voyages when on the short track.

Franklin and the IMM/White Star team in New York were pleased by the order, which meant *Olympic* should be able to steam fast enough on eastbound crossings to reach New York on Tuesday night.

When the next arrival was again on a Wednesday, Franklin expressed his disappointment to Ismay in a letter dated August 19, the day *Olympic* left New York on her sixth voyage.

I was sorry the *Olympic* did not dock on Tuesday, but am pleased with her Eastbound bookings.

Ismay replied on September 5:

Your sorrow that the *Olympic* did not dock on Tuesday night last voyage will, I hope, be mitigated by her docking on Tuesday this voyage, as we have just received a cable that at 9 o'clock last night she was 271 miles east of Nantucket, which we calculate would make her due at Ambrose Channel at 6 o'clock to-night, and I presume she will get up to the dock at about 10 o'clock, which will make an extremely comfortable (!!!) landing for her passengers, and I am sure they will much prefer this to dawdling away time and landing on Wednesday morning, to say nothing of their having had the pleasant uncertainty, from the time they left here, as to whether they would land on Tuesday evening, or not.

Preparing so large a ship in time was an on-going headache for Franklin and the company, but nothing compared to the colossal task that had just been dropped in his lap. Soon the whole world would be clamoring for word of *Titanic*'s fate and that of her passengers and crew, and the spotlight would shine unsparingly on Philip S. Franklin.

For the moment, Franklin was operating with an absence of information save those few reports that had been relayed to him by anxious reporters. Typically he did not receive updates from White Star steamers en route to New York. As a matter of course his office had been notified when *Titanic* departed Belfast after her sea trials, and when she arrived in Southampton.

As the ship sailed toward Queenstown, Franklin had sent a message to Bruce Ismay along the lines of 'Successful future to the *Titanic* and successful voyage also to yourself.'

From then on, he'd heard nothing, nor did he expect to. Perhaps when the ship approached New York waters on Tuesday, Ismay would send Franklin a message akin to the one he sent upon the completion of *Olympic*'s maiden voyage the previous June: '*Olympic* is a marvel.'

Franklin and his staff used what sparse information they had gleaned from press and company reports to chart the ships involved. *Titanic* was 1,080 miles from New

York, and *Olympic* was, they estimated, about 360 miles to the east of her sister ship at this moment.

'We had no communication at that time from any ship or anybody which in our opinion was authentic,' Franklin said. 'We had numerous rumors from all sources.'

With no information on which to act, Franklin's office continued to solicit information from news organizations, offices in Montreal and Halifax and from *Olympic*.

At about 6.00 a.m. local time, Franklin again wired *Olympic*: 'Keep us fully posted regarding *Titanic*.'

Haddock replied: 'Since midnight, when her position was 41.46 north, 50.14 west, have been unable to communicate. We are now 310 miles from her, 9 AM under full power. Will inform you at once if hear anything.'

Franklin had little information to share as New Yorkers awoke to the first news of *Titanic*'s collision. The news was meager and conflicting. There were three basic stories on the streets that morning: THE NEW *TITANIC* HIT BY ICEBERG, APPEALS FOR AID, SAYS WIRELESS REPORT (*The New York Herald*), ALL SAVED FROM *TITANIC* AFTER COLLISION (*The Evening Sun*) and NEW LINER *TITANIC* HITS AN ICEBERG; SINKING BY THE BOW AT MIDNIGHT; WOMEN PUT OFF IN LIFEBOATS; LAST WIRELESS AT 12:27 A.M. BLURRED (*The New York Times*).

Conflicting stories in city newspapers added to the anxiety of *Titanic* passengers' relatives and friends, and by 8 a.m. crowds were gathering outside White Star's Broadway office. Franklin and his colleagues were now overwhelmed by questions shouted from eager reporters and concerned New Yorkers.

Haddock would soon find himself in a similar situation. Now eight hours into his mad dash eastward, with no definitive information about *Titanic*, Haddock realized his careful efforts to keep the news from the bulk of his ship's company was about to unravel as *Olympic*'s passengers began to emerge from their cabins for breakfast.

It is not known how many passengers learned of the *Titanic*'s situation overnight – but certainly the Burnhams' experience in learning of the *Titanic*'s situation on Sunday night was exceptional. Most of their fellow passengers didn't learn about the collision – or their ship's race to the scene – until they awoke Monday morning.

Olympic's passengers got the first indication that things were amiss when they emerged on deck that morning. What they saw certainly aroused interest – and gossip. The lifeboats had been uncovered, swung out and made ready, ropes coiled, so that no time would be lost when *Olympic* reached her sister's side.

It was a similar scene – played out on the boat deck of the *Carpathia* just after midnight – that had alerted *Carpathia*'s passengers to their ship's change in course and destination, as Walter Lord wrote in *A Night to Remember*:[3]

... Mrs Louis M. Odgen awoke to a cold cabin and a speeding ship. Hearing loud noises overhead, she too decided something must be wrong. She shook her sleeping husband. His diagnosis didn't reassure her – the noise was the crew breaking out the chocks from the lifeboats overhead. He opened the stateroom door and saw a line of stewards carrying blankets and mattresses. Not very reassuring either.

On the *Olympic*, as on the *Carpathia*, it was the uncovering of the lifeboats that first aroused passengers' suspicions.

Soon, news of the tragedy spread from passenger to passenger throughout the ship as the *Olympic* continued her dash eastward. The American poet and journalist Ella Wheeler Wilcox, sixty-one, was dining with her husband, Robert, when word of *Titanic*'s peril reached them.

'At the breakfast table our steward told us that news had been received that the *Titanic* had struck an iceberg, but was saved with all on board,' Ella said. 'He said, however, he feared more serious news might come later.'[4]

Another writer, novelist R. H. Benson, got the news at the same time and was incredulous. He took to his diary to record the news, as if by writing it down, he could comprehend the unthinkable. 'On coming down from mass this morning I heard a sentence from a lift boy that made me wonder,' Benson wrote. 'I asked what was the matter and was told that the *Titanic* had communicated with us that she was in a sinking condition; that we were moving full speed towards her, and should probably arrive at about 3:30.'[5]

Not content with this information alone, Benson set out to learn more. After talking with stewards and 'various officials,' he also learned that *Olympic* had received the news between midnight and 1 a.m. At that time, the *Titanic* was sinking, and her passengers were taking to the boats. He also was told that two ships were already standing by – one being the White Star liner *Baltic*.

The impulse to record the historic event was not Benson's alone. Another passenger known only as Earl wrote a letter home Monday morning to share the news. 'The sea has quieted down some and the sun is shining today,' he wrote. '*Titanic*, a sister ship, is in distress off the coast of Newfoundland. We have altered our course since three o'clock this morning and we are racing to her at full speed. Are making 25 knots an hour and expect to reach her about three o'clock this afternoon.'

Leaving the *Olympic*'s spacious First Class Dining Saloon for a stroll on deck, Ella and Robert Wilcox encountered Robert's friend George Marcus of the New York firm Marcus & Company.

'Mr. Marcus and his artist son walked with us; Mr. Marcus recounted a curious dream he had had the previous afternoon,' Ella said. 'He said, "I told my son after waking from my afternoon nap, that I had dreamed of the *Titanic*. I thought I saw it sailing over a smooth sea, and then suddenly run up the sheer side of an enormous iceberg and turn a somersault and sink into the sea." The son said both he and his father felt the fate of the *Titanic* was more serious than had been reported.'[6]

Mr Marcus's premonition aside, the first reports to reach *Olympic*'s passengers and crew were optimistic. *Titanic* was injured, but her passengers were safe, and the *Olympic*, like many other ships, was rushing to her aid.

Olympic's passengers now discovered that stewards and stewardesses had worked overnight to prepare a number of beds for *Titanic*'s company, and word had been spread quietly that fresh water was to be used sparingly so there would be enough when *Titanic*'s passengers and crew were brought on board. That word now spread to passengers, too, who also joined in preparing staterooms and public rooms for additional passengers.

Actress Madame Simone, returning to Europe after a visit to America, was told that the *Titanic* had met with a slight accident, and that her passengers would be taken aboard *Olympic* once she reached the scene.

The news wasn't cause for alarm. In fact, Madame Simone remembered, it was quite the contrary.

> At this news there was increased gayety on the *Olympic*, and cabins were prepared for the expected guests as if it were a festive occasion. In fact, much happy enthusiasm was shown in anticipation of these casual meetings in midocean.[7]

When the Burnhams had learned of *Titanic*'s collision Sunday night, their first response had been to offer their cabin to their friends Frank Millet and Archibald Butt when *Olympic* reached *Titanic*'s side. The same impulse now spread throughout *Olympic* as passengers learned their ship was racing to aid the wounded sister ship.

A rumor began to spread on board *Olympic* that passengers were going to be mustered for a lifeboat drill. First Class passenger E. Marshall Fox, the European representative for the US Steel Corporation, had heard as much.[9] But such a drill never materialized. Haddock was taking great pains to avoid panic, and he would scarcely want to alert his passengers to his ship's severe shortage of lifeboats.

Another rumor would later be relayed to reporters when the ship reached shore. Revd R. H. Benson was among the passengers who heard through the grapevine that two ships had reached *Titanic* and were aiding in the evacuation.

'We were told that we were to take over the *Baltic*'s mail for England and that the *Baltic* would return to New York with the *Titanic*'s passengers,' Benson said. 'It was also stated that the *Carpathia* and another vessel in addition to the *Baltic* were cruising around the scene ...'

As the passengers gossiped about *Titanic* over breakfast, *Olympic*'s wireless operators reached out to Cape Race for more information but couldn't hear the reply. At 7.50 a.m., *Olympic* asked *Asian*: 'Can you give me any information *Titanic*, and if any ships standing by her?' A few minutes later, she asked *Scandinavian* the same question.

Then, at 8.30 a.m., *Asian* replied:

CAPTAIN, *Olympic*: *Asian* heard *Titanic* signaling Cape Race on and off from 8 to 10 p.m., local time, Sunday. Messages too faint to read. Finished calling SOS midnight. Position given as latitude 41.46 longitude, 50.14. No further information. *Asian* then 300 miles west of *Titanic* and towing oil tank to Halifax.

At 9 a.m., Franklin told reporters that even if *Titanic* had struck ice, her watertight compartments would keep her afloat until help arrived. 'We place absolute confidence in the *Titanic*. We believe that the boat is unsinkable.' He went on to say, 'There is no danger that the *Titanic* will sink. The boat is unsinkable, and nothing but inconvenience will be suffered by the passengers.'

SS *Parisian* signaled the *Olympic* with an update at 9.25 a.m. New York time:

I sent traffic to the *Titanic* at 8.30 last night and heard him send traffic to Cape Race just before I went to bed. I turned in at 11.15 ship's time. The *Californian* was about fifty miles astern of us. I heard the following this morning at six o'clock. According to information received the *Carpathia* has picked up about twenty boats with passengers. The *Baltic* is returning to give assistance. As regards *Titanic* have heard nothing. Don't know if she has sunk.

Haddock immediately forwarded the latest news to Franklin's office in New York: '*Parisian* reports *Carpathia* in attendance and picked up 20 boats of passengers and *Baltic* returning to give assistance. Position not given.'

The report failed to state that *Carpathia* had picked up the *only* survivors and kept hope alive that *Baltic* would soon be on the scene. Franklin was also getting conflicting reports about other ships that might have reached the scene in time to take on *Titanic* passengers.

Franklin replied:

HADDOCK, *Olympic*: April 15, 1912. Thanks your message. We have received nothing from *Titanic*, but rumored here that she is proceeding slowly Halifax, but we cannot confirm this. We expect *Virginian* alongside *Titanic*; try and communicate her.

Rumors continued to swirl outside White Star's offices, and while Franklin ignored the worst of them, he latched onto any positive news. When he heard the rumors about Halifax, he ordered a train be dispatched there immediately. Some relatives of *Titanic* passengers rushed to board the '*Titanic* Special' as it began the trek to Nova Scotia.

By mid-morning, Franklin and other IMM and line officials were busy greeting an ever-growing stream of callers – from Mrs Benjamin Guggenheim and J. P. Morgan, Jr, to the father of Mrs John Jacob Astor.

It was impossible to think of any real harm coming to the *Titanic*, and any positive news was generally believed. This was as true in England as it was in New York. One English woman would later recount a visit her mother had paid on April 15 to a school where her grandmother was headmistress:[10]

... they went into this one class and grandmother said, "Stand up any child who has a relative on the *Titanic*" and the whole class stood up. And one little mite said, "Oh, there's no need to worry, Miss, the *Olympic* is rushing to her aid."

Realizing that his passengers were aware of *Titanic*'s collision, Captain Haddock now saw to it that they were kept updated even though information was, for the moment, scant and conflicting.

Just before noon, as passengers were sitting down for lunch, a bulletin was posted in red ink in the First Class Smoking Room and the First Class Reading and Writing Room. It was as reassuring as it was brief: 'New York reports all *Titanic* passengers safe.'[8]

First Class Passenger Roy W. Howard, General Manager of United Press Associations, included this update in a wireless message he intended to send to his associates on shore, but the ship's purser said it would be impossible 'because the wireless was being utilized to its fullest capacity to get news of the tragedy' and to 'communicate with the *Titanic.*'

W. Orton Tewson was also making notes, and as he later reported for *The New York Times*, 'This welcome news snapped the tension on the *Olympic*, but still the liner continued the furious race to the *Titanic* with every furnace going and fifty extra volunteer stokers working below.'

Indeed, the news 'all *Titanic* passengers safe' was being reported on both sides of the Atlantic Monday, offering some reassurance to worried relatives and White Star employees. For the *Olympic*, the truth was still hundreds of miles, and a few hours, away.

As *Olympic* continued to race to the scene, iceberg warnings came in from *Asian* and *Mesaba*. Having received the warnings, Captain Haddock reached out to captains nearer the scene to ask about the safest route to proceed.

At 12.25 p.m. New York time, Haddock asked the *Parisian*:

Can we steer 41.22 north, 50.14 west from westward, and then north to *Titanic* fairly free from ice. We are due there midnight. Should appreciate *Titanic*'s correct position if you can give it me. HADDOCK

Parisian's captain replied at 12.50 p.m.:

Safe from field ice to 41.22. 50.14; as the ice was yesterday, you would need to steer from that position about northeast and north to about lat. 41.42 and 50, then approach his position from the westward, steering about west north-west. My knowledge of the *Titanic*'s position at midnight was derived from your own message to New York, in which you gave it as 41.47, 50.20; if such were correct, she would be in heavy field ice and numerous bergs. Hope and trust matters are not as bad as they appear.

Franklin was hoping the same thing. He sent another message to Haddock with a request: 'Endeavor ascertain where Ismay is. Advise me and convey him deepest sympathy from us all. FRANKLIN'

Olympic lies at anchor at quarantine upon her arrival in New York. 'We knew the excitement would be unprecedented and that our early morning arrival off quarantine would be more hectic than usual,' said stewardess Violet Jessop. (William H. Rau Collection)

With an excited stream of escorts whistling at her arrival, *Olympic* steams up the Hudson River in New York harbor. In the foreground is the White Star Line pier, which had just been extended in order to accommodate the biggest ship in the world. (Library of Congress)

With *Lusitania* passing behind her, *Olympic* is eased into her berth by tugs. Passengers line her decks to witness the triumphant arrival. (Library of Congress)

June 21, 1911: *Olympic* arrived at the entrance to her pier in New York City on the successful completion of her maiden voyage. 'Such a greeting she got! And such a seraphic smile as her commander wore!' wrote one newspaper of the occasion. (Library of Congress)

Airplane pilot Tom Sopwith flew low over *Olympic* as she departed New York Harbor for the first time in order to drop a parcel on the ship's decks. The package, which reportedly carried a message to Captain Smith and a passenger's eyeglasses, missed its mark and sank in the harbor. (Library of Congress)

In this magazine advertisement of the period, *Olympic*'s draw among the wealthy is used to sell overcoats for Hart Schaffner & Marx. (Author's Collection)

WOVEN IN SILK,
R.M.S. OLYMPIC.

Length 883 feet.   Breadth 92½ feet.   Tonnage 46359.   Speed 22½ knots.

An unusual view of the *Olympic*, woven in silk. (J & C McCutcheon Collection)

A brochure extolling the virtues of *Olympic*, 'The Ship Magnificent'. (J & C McCutcheon Collection)

 **S.S. OLYMPIC 45000 TONS**

White Star publicists illustrated *Olympic*'s size by comparing her to the largest man-made structures of the day. (J & C McCutcheon Collection)

An early view of *Olympic* in Southampton Water with an abundance of passengers clearly visible on her stern. (J & C McCutcheon Collection)

On her return maiden voyage, tugs and tenders brought passengers, cargo and mails to *Olympic* in Cherbourg, France, where the harbor was not deep enough to receive so large a ship. (J & C McCutcheon Collection)

An early portrait of *Olympic* as she executes a turn near land. (D. Pare Collection)

Olympic in New York waters in 1911. (J & C McCutcheon Collection)

Olympic makes an interesting contrast to the city skyline as she enters New York after a 1911 voyage. (William H. Rau Collection)

Olympic was carrying a record number of passengers to New York at the end of the summer season when the collision occurred, leaving a nasty gash in her side that necessitated her return to Southampton, and later Belfast, for repairs. (J & C McCutcheon Collection)

Hawke's bow shows significant damage as she returns to Southampton harbor after the collision with *Olympic*. (J & C McCutcheon Collection)

An artist's rendition of the collision between *Olympic* and the British cruiser *Hawke*. (J & C McCutcheon Collection)

Another view of the damage caused by *Hawke* to the *Olympic*. (J & C McCutcheon Collection)

Olympic returned to Southampton under her own steam after the collision with *Hawke*. The damage (outlined in white near her stern) extended below the waterline and seemed to underscore the infallibility of the ship's watertight compartments. Among her inconvenienced passengers was Harry Widener, who in less than a year would die while sailing home on *Titanic*. (J & C McCutcheon Collection)

Olympic departs Ocean Dock on another westbound voyage to America. (J & C McCutcheon Collection)

The day after their engagement was announced, Madeleine Force and John Jacob Astor were photographed outside his New York City mansion. In the scandal that followed their September 1911 wedding, the couple fled for Europe in January 1912 on *Olympic*. (Library of Congress)

When *Olympic* (at left) returned to Harland & Wolff for replacement of a lost propeller blade in March 1912, *Titanic* experienced another delay in her fitting out. This was the last time the two sister ships were photographed together. (J & C McCutcheon Collection)

Completed after several delays caused by her sister ship, *Olympic*, *Titanic* rested in Ocean Dock on Good Friday, April 5 1912, just five days before her departure for New York. Her final design included several improvements over the *Olympic*, including the installation of glass windows in the forward part of A Deck to protect passengers from ocean spray. (Author's Collection)

CHAPTER 8
The Awful Truth

By 1 p.m. Monday, *Olympic*'s captain and wireless operators were becoming increasingly frustrated by the lack of new information about the stricken *Titanic*. Signals from Cape Race were weak and hard to decipher, and the messages that were coming through were being jammed by the proximity of the German liner *Berlin*.[1]

When messages finally did come through, they contained not news but rather requests for news from media outlets in New York and beyond. 'Will pay you liberally for story of rescue of *Titanic*'s passengers,' read one. Another offered thirty pounds per column. Yet another said the operators could 'Name your own price.'

Irritated by the requests, which asked them to violate Marconi rules, *Olympic*'s operators contacted Cape Race: 'It's no use sending messages from newspapers asking us for news of *Titanic* as we have none to give.'

The lack of news was frustrating for everyone – from worried relatives of *Titanic* passengers and crew to the company that sold them transatlantic passage, not to mention crews of vessels now racing to the scene.

Captain Haddock was put in a particularly difficult position. His ship had the closest bond to *Titanic* and the most powerful wireless set on the Atlantic. If anyone had the capability to get the full story, it should have been him. Yet after 13 hours spent racing through the night, sending inquiries by wireless all the while, Haddock had more questions than answers. His most pressing question, however, was about to be answered.

Olympic began calling *Carpathia*, a ship that by all accounts already had reached *Titanic*'s position and rescued passengers in lifeboats, and finally got a terse reply at 3.50 p.m. ship time.

'Steady on. I don't do everything at once. Patience please,' came the reply from *Carpathia*'s operator, Harold Cottam, who had been working at his set ceaselessly since receiving *Titanic*'s cry for help the previous night.

Then came the awful news, from Cottam's key to the *Olympic* operator's ears.

I received distress signals from the *Titanic* at 11.20, and we proceeded right to the spot mentioned. On arrival at daybreak we saw field ice 25 miles, apparently solid, and a quantity of wreckage and a number of boats full of people. We raised about 670 souls.

The *Titanic* has sunk. She went down in about two hours. Captain and all engineers lost. Our captain sent order that there was no need for *Baltic* to come any farther. So with that she returned on her course to Liverpool. Are you going to resume your course on that information? We have two or three officers aboard and the second Marconi operator, who had been creeping his way through water 30° sometime. Mr Ismay aboard.

Moore immediately relayed *Carpathia*'s message to Cape Race and would later be asked to explain why the news had not reached Franklin in New York for another two hours.

I at once cleared both messages to Cape Race and, speaking from memory, it was certainly not after 4 p.m. (2 p.m. New York time) when Cape Race had the news. What delay occurred in transmitting the message by the land lines to New York, if any, I cannot say.[2]

The message was immediately taken to Captain Haddock on *Olympic*'s bridge by the junior wireless operator.

While the rest of the world would soon be clamoring for news from the little Cunarder, and raging when it wasn't forthcoming, Moore and Bagot were impressed with Cottam's dedication to the task at hand.

Moore thanked Cottam for the messages and assured him that, 'Any urgent messages for shore we will send through Cape Race for you, but please stand by for service (ship to ship) messages.'

Cottam replied: 'OK, old man, but I'm tired and hungry. Have had nothing to eat since 5.30 p.m. yesterday.'

On *Olympic*'s bridge, Bagot handed the latest message to Captain Haddock.

Carpathia's message was a terrible shock to Captain Haddock, who had worked with many of *Titanic*'s officers and knew a great many of her crew personally. A mere two weeks ago, he had traded commands with Captain Smith.

Titanic was gone. The shock of that news – unthinkable as it was – was made worse by the fact that no ship had reached the sinking ship in time to be of assistance to those trapped on board.

The only hope for *Titanic*'s passengers were her twenty lifeboats – which held space for roughly half the number of people on board.

Those fortunate enough to find a seat in a lifeboat watched the horror of the sinking and, when it was over, endured the screams of the dying, an unearthly wail that lasted for more than half an hour. Some survivors later said that as bad as the cries had been, the silence that followed was worse.

The suffering of those in the boats, like those in the water, would be short-lived, however. *Carpathia*'s rockets were sighted from the lifeboats within an hour of the final plunge, and at 4 a.m., less than two hours after *Titanic* disappeared, the little Cunarder came to a stop when a light from lifeboat 2 was sighted. Within minutes, the first survivors were being taken aboard, with the able-bodied climbing a rope ladder dropped down the ship's side. Others were lifted on board in a canvas sack.

The first surviving officer to board the ship, Fourth Officer Joseph Boxhall, reported to *Carpathia*'s bridge and informed her captain that *Titanic* had foundered at 2:20 a.m.

Some of *Carpathia*'s passengers gathered at the rails and watched the rescue as it happened. Mabel Fenwick, who was celebrating her honeymoon on *Carpathia*, had hid on deck as the ship sped toward this scene. Her stealthiness was now rewarded with a front row seat to history as she snapped photos of *Titanic*'s lifeboats coming alongside the rescue ship.

If only *Olympic* had been here in *Carpathia*'s place, a number of happy reunions would now be taking place like the one enjoyed between Charles Marshall and his nieces. Awakened by a knock on his cabin door, Marshall asked, 'What is it?'

A *Carpathia* steward answered, 'Your niece wants to see you, sir.'

Marshall was confused. His three nieces were crossing on the *Titanic*. In fact, they had sent him a wireless message last night. How could they be on the *Carpathia*? He opened the door and there was his niece, Mrs E. D. Appleton. Soon the other nieces were with them as they had their unexpected family reunion in mid-ocean.[3]

Happy reunions were in short supply. Many of the women who had boarded lifeboats expected to be reunited with their husbands, loved ones and friends when they reached the rescue ship. At 8:30 a.m., as the last survivor – Second Officer Charles Lightoller – climbed the rope ladder, the realization came that in most cases, no such reunion would take place.

Captain Rostron and his crew had conducted an exemplary rescue, and at 9 a.m., with all *Titanic* survivors on board and thirteen of her lifeboats stowed on board, *Carpathia*'s crew performed another sad duty – a service of remembrance for those who had died and one of thanksgiving for those who had been saved.

When the service concluded, *Carpathia* got underway for New York as the arduous task of compiling the list of survivors began.

Having delivered the awful news to the captain, *Olympic*'s junior wireless operator returned to the wireless cabin with a message from Captain Haddock to *Carpathia*'s Captain Rostron, which was transmitted at 2.35 p.m. New York Time: '7.12 p.m. G.M.T. our position 41.17 N 53.53 W steering east true. Shall I meet you and where?'

At that moment, *Carpathia* had stopped her engines in order to perform a solemn service – committing four *Titanic* victims to the deep. The victims, two crew members and two passengers, had died of exposure in lifeboats before being brought aboard the rescue ship. Now, their bodies were wrapped, weighted and returned to the sea as prayers were offered.

Carpathia replied: 'Captain *Olympic* – 7 30 GMT lat. 41.15 N long. 51.45 W, am steering south 87 West true. Returning to New York with *Titanic*'s passengers – Rostron.'

Olympic was to the west of *Carpathia*'s course at a distance of roughly 110 miles. She had come so close to *Titanic*'s last known position – so close …

The crushing news of *Titanic*'s sinking had dashed Haddock's hopes of reaching the scene in time to be of assistance, but he still hoped to play a role in returning survivors to shore.

In a series of short replies, however, *Carpathia*'s captain rejected with growing vehemence the idea of transferring survivors to the sister ship.

CAPTAIN *Olympic*: Bruce Ismay is under opiate. ROSTRON. *Carpathia*

CAPTAIN *Olympic*: Do you think it is advisable *Titanic*'s passengers see *Olympic*? Personally I say not. ROSTRON. *Carpathia*

After checking with Ismay, who had isolated himself in the cabin of *Carpathia*'s doctor, Rostron sent the following:

CAPTAIN *Olympic*: Mr. Ismay orders *Olympic* not to be seen by *Carpathia*. No transfer to take place. ROSTRON

Haddock conceded the idea of a mid-ocean transfer of *Titanic* survivors to her nearly identical sister ship was inadvisable, but he was not ready to abandon all hope of rescuing more *Titanic* passengers. Haddock was still reluctant to believe the worse.

CAPTAIN *Carpathia*: Kindly inform me if there is the slightest hope of searching *Titanic* position at daybreak. Agree with you on not meeting. Will stand on present course until you have passed and will then haul more to southward. Does this parallel of 41.17 N. lead clear of the ice? Have you communicated the disaster to our people at New York or Liverpool, or shall I do so, and what particulars can you give me to send? Sincere thanks for what you have done. HADDOCK

Carpathia's reply:

CAPT. HADDOCK, *Olympic*:
South point pack ice 41.16 north. Don't attempt to go north until 49.30 west. Many bergs, large and small, amongst pack. Also for many miles to eastward. Fear absolutely no hope searching *Titanic*'s position. Left Leyland SS *Californian* searching around. All boats accounted for. About 675 souls saved, crew and passengers; latter nearly all women and children. *Titanic* foundered about 2.20 a. m., 5.47 GMT, in 41.46 north. 50.14 west; not certain of having got through. Please forward to White Star, also to Cunard, Liverpool and New York, that I am returning to New York. Consider this most advisable for many considerations. ROSTRON.

At 4:35 p.m. ship time, Haddock passed the official word of *Titanic*'s fate to White Star via the station at Cape Race.

ISMAY, New York and Liverpool: *Carpathia* reached *Titanic* position at daybreak. Found boats and wreckage only. *Titanic* had foundered about 2.20 a. m. in 41.16 N., 50.14 W. All her boats accounted for. About 675 souls saved, crew and passengers; latter nearly all women and children. Leyland Line SS *Californian* remaining and searching position of disaster. *Carpathia* returning to New York with survivors. Please inform Cunard. HADDOCK. *Olympic*.

It was official, concise and to the point – and the news could not be put off any longer. But it was impersonal, and given Haddock's grief, it would not do. He followed the official message with his own personal message to Franklin's office in New York:

> Inexpressible sorrow. Am proceeding straight on voyage. *Carpathia* informs me no hope in searching. Will send names survivors as obtainable. Yamsi on *Carpathia*. HADDOCK.

Yamsi was the long-accepted company code for Ismay.

As W. Orton Tewson would later report for *The New York Times*, this was the moment when *Olympic*'s passengers noticed the ship was 'making a swerve' and had 'turned her head homeward on the old course.'[4]

'Still,' he wrote, 'no further alarm was felt for it was generally believed that the shipwrecked passengers and crew had all been picked up by other vessels, and that the *Olympic* had only turned away because her help was no longer needed.'

As Franklin would later testify to the US Senate Inquiry, the latest message from Haddock, the one that confirmed *Titanic* had foundered, was handed to him by his assistant at about 6:20 p.m., four minutes after it had arrived in the New York office.

> … it was such a terrible shock that it took us a few minutes to get ourselves together. Then at once I telephoned, myself, to two of our directors, Mr Steele and Mr Morgan, Jr, and at the same time sent downstairs for the reporters. I started to read the message, holding it in my hands, to the reporters. I got off the first line and a half, where it said, "The *Titanic* sank at 2 o'clock a.m.," and there was not a reporter left in the room – they were so anxious to get out to telephone the news.

The reporters' sudden departure gave Franklin time to cope with his own shock, which would last for hours as he continued to hold out hope that while the ship had sunk, other ships might have saved additional *Titanic* passengers and crew.

The Leyland liner *Californian*, whose wireless operator had switched off shortly before *Titanic* began sending her distress signals, and whose captain, Stanley Lord, failed to act after his officers reporting seeing *Titanic*'s rockets being fired throughout the night, had heard of *Titanic*'s loss Monday morning and steamed for her last reported position.

At 4.50 p.m., *Olympic*'s operators asked Cottam of the *Carpathia* to send his list of survivors, but before the transfer of information could begin, *Californian* broke in with her own update:

> We were the second boat on the scene of disaster. All we could see there were some boxes and coats and a few empty boats and what looked like oil on the water. When we were near the *Carpathia* he would not answer me, though I kept on calling him, as I wanted the position. He kept on talking to the *Baltic*. The latter says he is going to report me for jamming. We were the nearer boat to the *Carpathia*. A boat called the *Birma* was still looking.

Californian called *Olympic* again at 5.20 p.m. to share an ice report. A few minutes later, *Carpathia*'s Captain Rostron sends a private message to Haddock that added to the latter's considerable grief:

> Captain: Chief, first, and sixth officers, and all engineers gone; also doctor; all pursers; one Marconi operator, and chief steward gone. We have second, third, fourth and fifth officers and one Marconi operator on board. ROSTRON.

Carpathia's wireless operator didn't have a partner, but *Titanic*'s surviving operator, Harold Bride, would soon assist him in transmitting the list of survivors. *Cottam*'s exhaustion was clear, and he reminded Bagot and Moore to 'Please excuse sending but am half asleep.'

Realizing that *Olympic*'s primary mission now was to act as relay station, Captain Haddock saw to the comfort of his own wireless operators, who were now taking turns at the key, by assigning an able bodied seaman to the wireless cabin. Stationed just inside the door, the seaman attended to Moore and Bagot as they continued their work.

As Cottam sent word of *Titanic*'s senior officers, he identified them only by rank. But to the recipients on *Olympic*, the men all had names and, in most cases, personal histories that were well-known. Haddock was devastated.

E. J. Smith was commodore of the fleet and, in Haddock's estimation, a fine captain. Most of the officers who had followed E. J. to *Titanic* were now gone, and while the precise circumstances of the catastrophe wouldn't be known to him until he reached England, Haddock now understood that most of his friends were gone.

Indeed, each name brought a new pang of sadness.

Titanic's first officer, William Murdoch, who was at the helm when she struck the iceberg, had worked under Captain Haddock when he was master of the *Cedric* in 1906, just before Haddock assumed command of *Oceanic*. And *Titanic*'s chief purser, Hugh McElroy, had also been with Haddock on *Cedric*.

Cedric was a happy memory for Haddock; she was the first new ship under his command, and he'd had the honor of taking her on the maiden voyage. McElroy was well-suited to his duties as purser, with a knack for conflict resolution and a calm, friendly demeanor that endeared him to passengers. It was these very qualities that led Captain Smith to insist that McElroy join him on the new *Titanic*.

In his *Cedric* days, McElroy had a pet parrot that provided levity on board ship. McElroy had adopted the bird from a fellow crewman on White Star's old *Britannic* when McElroy was on the South African run. The owner gave him the bird on the condition that he name it 'Baden-Powell' after the well-known lieutenant-general of the British Army.[5]

Purser McElroy kept 'Baden-Powell' in his cabin or on his broad shoulder when walking the decks. The avian adventures of the purser and his parrot were soon the subject of a feature in *The New York Times*:

> When the *Cedric* arrived at New York on her last trip Badin-Powell was not on deck when the big liner was berthed. Neither was his guardian. When found he was perched on McElroy's shoulder, the officer being busy in his office getting his

papers ready to be turned over to the proper officials. An acquaintance of McElroy's knocked at the door.

"Keep out. No lobsters wanted," was what the knocker on the outside heard from within.

"Shut up, Baden. Come in: it's all right," answered McElroy, and the friend opened the door.

McElroy greeted his friend warmly, while Baden-Powell, with a look of disdain on his peaked countenance, eyed him critically.

"Bum looker; don't cut much ice," piped the parrot.

McElroy told the bird to ship up, whereupon Baden-Powell gave a loud "All right, all right" and leaving his place on McElroy's shoulder, took up his position on the windowsill overlooking the grand stairway.

"Look out, Mac: the old man's coming," said Baden-Powell.

"I told you to shup up," retorted the purser.

"All right," answered Baden-Powell, and he obeyed orders.

Haddock knew McElroy, and the other men on Rostron's list, to be the best the White Star Line had to offer. One moment they'd been at the peak of their careers, sailing on the newest, biggest ship in the fleet. Now they were gone. It was difficult to comprehend.

Olympic's leading fireman was stunned – not only by the unthinkable disaster that had sent *Titanic* to the bottom – but by the appalling loss of life. 'After 4 o'clock on Monday came the awful message. I knew then how hopeless our efforts were. I have lost myself over fifty close friends, many of them old school mates.'

Rostron soon sent another message to assure *Olympic* that his ship 'Will send names immediately we can. You can understand we are working under considerable difficulty. Everything possible being done for comfort of survivors. Please maintain Stanbi. ROSTRON.'

Having already faced journalists in order to deliver the main headline – that *Titanic* was gone – Franklin now needed more information to complete the story. At 7.10 p.m., he wired *Olympic* to state: 'It is vitally important that we have name of every survivor on *Carpathia* immediately. If you can expedite this by standing by *Carpathia*, kindly do so. FRANKLIN'

The request was well-timed – *Olympic* had just received at least a partial list of survivors.

Within minutes of his last request, Franklin sent a message to Haddock:

Distressed to learn from your message the *Carpathia* is only steamer with passengers. Understood *Virginian* and *Parisian* also had passengers. Are you in communication with them, and can you get any information? FRANKLIN

As if to clarify his hopes, Franklin followed his message with another:

Wire us with name of every passenger, officer, and crew on *Carpathia*. It is most important. Keep in communication with *Carpathia* until you accomplish this.

Instruct *Californian* to stand by scene of wreck until she hears from us or is relieved or her coal supply runs short. Ascertain *Californian* coal and how long she can stand by. Have life rafts been accounted for? Are you absolutely satisfied that *Carpathia* has all survivors, as had rumor that *Virginian* and *Parisian* also have survivors. Where is *Baltic*? FRANKLIN

Franklin was still clinging to hope that other ships might have reached the scene in time to help *Titanic*'s passengers and crew. When he next faced reporters at 8 p.m., Franklin refused to speculate on the number of lives lost and said only that *Olympic*'s message 'neglected to say that all the crew had been saved.'[6]

At 8.15 p.m., with no reply from *Olympic*, his hope dimmed as he conceded that 'Probably a number of lives have been lost.'

At 8.25 p.m., *Olympic* asked *Carpathia* if the list of third class passengers and crew was ready for transmission. The reply was: 'No; will send them soon.' In 1912, rigid social barriers meant that even now, third class passengers would come last in the pecking order. They had been last to reach the lifeboats, if they reached them at all, and now their relatives would have the longest wait to find out if they had lived or died.

While *Carpathia* seemed confident that she was the only ship carrying *Titanic* survivors, this was not clear to *Olympic*'s captain, and soon calls went out to other ships asking if they had any survivors on board.

In a private message transmitted at 8.35 p.m., *Olympic* discretely asked *Californian* if she had any *Titanic* passengers or crew on board. The answer was no.

At 8.45, just as *Olympic* began transmitting the partial list of survivors to shore, the *Californian* replied that she did not have any of *Titanic*'s complement of passengers or crew. At that same moment, Franklin was telling reporters that 'We very much fear there has been a great loss of life.'

Weeping openly by 9 p.m., Franklin admitted the worst: that *Titanic* had sunk with a 'horrible loss of life.' He shared his shock with the gathered press: 'I thought her unsinkable, and I based my opinion on the best expert advice. I do not understand it.'

At 9.55 p.m. Franklin wired *Olympic* again, this time to ensure that the work of relaying the list of survivors to shore would continue unabated.

Don't leave *Carpathia* until you have wired us the names of survivors or you have arranged for somebody else to immediately telegraph us the names. FRANKLIN

Half an hour later, *Olympic* got the OK from Sable Island and began transmitting the list of survivors. The world had just learned that the *Titanic* had indeed gone to the bottom and would in short order learn whom among her 2,228 passengers and crew she took with her, The sad duty of delivering the tragic news had fallen to her sister ship *Olympic*, onto which so many hopes of rescue had been placed.

On April 10, 1912, *Olympic* made her last arrival in New York as the world's biggest ship. Her sister, *Titanic*, had just departed Southampton earlier in the day and was expected to reach this same pier the following week. (Library of Congress)

Olympic's passengers line her decks to greet well-wishers at pier-side as the ship docks on April 10, 1912. Three days later the ship will depart again, leaving the pier for her sister ship, *Titanic*, which was expected on April 17. (Library of Congress)

Marconi Operator at Work in the Marconi Room of a Large Liner

A drawing of a ship's wireless room, based on the design used on the *Olympic*-class liners. (J & C McCutcheon Collection)

First class passenger Daniel Burnham, the famed architect who was perhaps best known as the man who oversaw the design and construction of the Chicago World's Fair in 1893, was among the first of *Olympic*'s passengers to learn of the *Titanic*'s distress calls. (Author's Collection)

A portrait of Harold Bride, one of *Titanic*'s wireless operators. (J & C McCutcheon Collection)

Harold Bride had to be carried off the *Carpathia* when she arrived at New York as his feet had been badly frost-bitten. (Library of Congress)

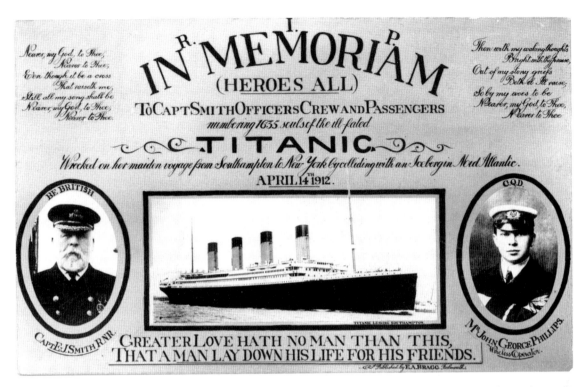

Titanic's other wireless operator, Jack Phillips, pictured on a commemorative postcard together with Captain Smith. (J & C McCutcheon Collection)

A close-up of the portrait of Jack Phillips.
(J & C McCutcheon Collection)

Frank Millet was a noted artist at whose insistence Major Butt had travelled to Europe. The old friends were returning to the US on board the *Titanic*. He is seen here together with a bookplate, an example of his work. (Author's Collection)

Major Archibald Butt had travelled to Europe at the insistence of Frank Millet, who was worried about the health of his friend. By the spring of 1912 Butt was close to suffering a mental breakdown over his conflicting allegiance to President Taft and Teddy Roosevelt. (Author's Collection)

Major Archibald Butt enjoyed the comforts of his stateroom, B-38, on *Titanic*'s port side. The Burnhams' cabin on *Olympic*, C63–65, would have been quite similar. (Author's Collection)

Novelist R. H. Benson overheard a conversation on board *Olympic* early on the morning of April 15, 1912, while boarding one of the ship's elevators after mass. Benson asked the elevator operator what was the matter and was told 'the *Titanic* had communicated with us that she was in a sinking condition; that we were moving full speed towards her.' (Author's Collection)

IMM vice president Philip Franklin received a call early on the morning of April 15 from an Associated Press reporter who asked for comment on reports that the *Titanic* had struck an iceberg and was sinking. 'Don't call me again with such silly information,' Franklin replied. (Library of Congress)

As early and conflicting reports began to arrive on April 15, crowds gathered in front of the White Star Line's offices in New York City. The steamship company didn't confirm the *Titanic*'s sinking until late that evening upon receiving the news from *Olympic* in mid-ocean. (Library of Congress)

The ladies on *Olympic* received updates on the *Titanic* from posted notices in the Reading and Writing Room. (William J. Rau Collection)

Madame Casimir-Perier, more popularly known as the actress Madame Simone, recalled the excitement she and her fellow passengers felt as they made *Olympic* cabins and public rooms ready to receive *Titanic*'s passengers and crew. (Author's Collection)

Poet Emma Wheeler Wilcox and her husband were strolling *Olympic*'s decks on April 15, 1912, when they encountered a friend who shared a dream he had the day before in which the *Titanic* struck an iceberg and sank. (Author's Collection)

Olympic lies in her Southampton berth shortly after the *Titanic* disaster. Mystery surrounds the flotilla of lifeboats floating nearby. It has been suggested that these may be *Titanic*'s lifeboats, brought back to England to be fitted onto the sister ship. (J & C McCutcheon Collection)

Olympic's Captain Haddock (third from left) was notoriously publicity-shy and found himself in the spotlight when compelled to testify at the US Senate's investigation into the *Titanic* disaster. (Author's Collection)

Captain Haddock's previous commands included the liner *Brittanic*, seen here painted white in 1900. (J & C McCutcheon Collection)

Oceanic was Captain Haddock's last command before he was transferred to the *Olympic*-class ships. (J & C McCutcheon Collection)

White Star hastily pressed *Olympic* back into service just three days after her return to England. More than 1,400 passengers lined her decks as the ship departed Southampton on the morning of April 24, a mere ten days after *Titanic* struck the iceberg. It was an impressive turn-around, but the voyage was not to be. (Courtesy Günter Bäbler)

On what would have been her first voyage following the *Titanic*'s loss, *Olympic* was stopped outbound from Southampton as a group of firemen and greasers went on strike over their contention that hastily added collapsible boats were not seaworthy. The *Olympic* was forced to return to port, and the voyage was cancelled. (J & C McCutcheon Collection)

Just two years after the *Titanic* disaster, *Olympic* and Captain Haddock were finally able to perform a rescue operation – this time for HMS *Audacious*, which had struck a mine in the Irish Sea. (J & C McCutcheon Collection)

Olympic in Southampton's floating dock allows an appreciation of her full proportions – and the full complement of lifeboats she was required to carry following the loss of her sister ship, *Titanic*. (J & C McCutcheon Collection)

Olympic in the dazzle paint that was meant to confuse German submarines. By the end of the war, *Olympic* had carried more troops than any other large liner (some estimates go as high as 200,000), earning her the nickname 'Old Reliable'. (J & C McCutcheon Collection)

In her post-war career, *Olympic* proved that her attractiveness to transatlantic passengers had not diminished, and she remained as popular as ever. (J & C McCutcheon Collection)

By the 1930s circumstances had converged to spell *Olympic*'s doom, including the merger of the Cunard and White Star lines, her unfortunate collision with the Nantucket lightship and the onset of the Great Depression. (J & C McCutcheon Collection)

It was the end of an era as *Olympic* sailed into the Tyne on October 13 1935 for her demolition. By this time the ship had been stripped of much of her interior furnishings and décor, which were sold at auction prior to her last departure from Southampton. (J & C McCutcheon Collection)

CHAPTER 9

The Ship is in Gloom

Olympic's passengers had carried their best hopes for *Titanic*, her passengers and crew through one last gathering together – Monday night's dinner. Immediately following the meal, however, they emerged from the ship's various dining rooms to find that a new bulletin had been posted.

As United Press Associations General Manager Roy W. Howard would report it later, the bulletin announced that *Titanic* 'had been totally destroyed and that all of her company had gone to the bottom with the exception of 675 who were then on the *Carpathia*.'

The New York Times later reported that, 'On the instant a hush fell over the ship with great sorrow, which was all the sharper and more poignant because it had followed a period of seven hours of joy and relief among those who did not share the tragic secret.'[1]

The novelist Revd R. H. Benson took to his diary again, noting the latest development:

6:30 p.m. - We have been receiving various messages – e.g. that all passengers were saved – this from New York – but now we have heard that only 675 are saved, crew and passengers, and that the passengers are chiefly women and children.[2]

Benson wasn't the sole diary keeper among *Olympic's* passengers, who now found themselves unwitting witnesses to history. Architect Daniel Burnham had been among the first to learn of *Titanic's* collision and now returned to his diary to record the latest news:

Later in the day we learned via Marconi, that she had struck an iceberg and had gone down; ... My Chief of Decoration of the Fair of 1893 and Vice-chairman of the Commission of Fine Arts, Frank D. Millet, whom I loved, was aboard of her, and with him was Major Archibald Butt, President Taft's military secretary. Their names are not on the list of survivors and probably they have gone down, thus cutting off my connection with one of the best fellows of the Fair.[3]

The news was stunning and in an instant shattered forever the excitement *Olympic's* passengers had felt at the thought of rescuing *Titanic's* passengers and crew.

Actress Madame Simone remembered the shock of that initial posting: '...We learned by a notice posted up that our course toward Europe had been resumed, and that the *Titanic* had foundered, only a few hundred persons escaping.'

'It seemed as if one single cry went up from the whole ship,' Madame Simone further recalled. 'I heard shrieks and sobs all around me. A majority of the passengers had friends or relatives on the *Titanic*, and the stewardesses had husbands or sisters working there. The people met each other silently and with reddened eyes, and dared not speak to each other and ask for news.'

All for the best, perhaps, as news was scarce and, when it did come, altogether heart-wrenching.

The poet Ella Wheeler Wilcox would later describe hearing 'the terrible facts' that afternoon, and the effect the news had on *Olympic*'s passengers and crew. 'It made the remainder of our voyage very gruesome indeed, as nearly all the crew and half the passengers had friends and relatives on the *Titanic*. Our room steward lost his father and two brothers.'⁴

Olympic's passengers and crew wouldn't get the whole truth, however, for two reasons. First, Captain Haddock wasn't getting the full story himself. Secondly, Haddock was filtering those few details that did come through in order to avoid a panic on board. After all, this was the nearly identical sister ship to a vessel that had just sunk with an appalling loss of life. The fewer details offered, the better.

The same impulse to minimize panic that had guided Captain Smith in *Titanic*'s last hours also dictated the way Captain Haddock would manage information for the remainder of the voyage.

While he knew the central truth could not be withheld, Haddock shared precious few details. In the absence of real information, *Olympic*'s passengers and crew were left to speculate.

A pall came over the ship, leaving passengers and crew in a haze as dense as the confusion regarding the disaster itself. Normal shipboard routine was suspended out of respect for *Titanic*'s dead.

Life on board a liner was normally lively and loud until late into the evening, but tonight *Olympic* was unusually quiet. The ship herself was quiet, nearly standing still as her wireless operators continued to transmit the list of *Titanic* survivors to wireless stations on shore.

The next morning, passengers awoke to new horrors. The shock of *Titanic*'s loss was still fresh, and on Tuesday *Olympic*'s company was met with a partial list of survivors, having been received by the ship overnight, that was posted at intervals as new names arrived.

Passengers and crew scanned the lists for loved ones on board the *Titanic* and, in most cases, were left with worry as the sought-after names were nowhere to be found.

Daniel Burnham anxiously awaited news of his friends aboard *Titanic* – Millet and Butt – and recorded his angst in his diary entry for that Tuesday morning.

Breakfasted in our rooms. Went out and read list of *Titanic*'s survivors telegraphed from the *Carpathia*, which is carrying them to New York. Frank's name is not among them, nor is Archie Butt's. My Steward is in grief; his son was a steward on the *Titanic* and has gone down. This ship is in gloom; everybody has lost friends, and some of them near relations.⁵

Burnham's wife was also actively maintaining a diary of events on board ship:

Heard the *Carpathia* had gone to their rescue as the *Titanic* had struck an iceberg – ship is in gloom! Many have friends aboard *Titanic*. At early hour word came *Titanic* had gone down very quickly, but still there is little known. Wire from Albert Wells nothing heard of Mr Wells [about Millet]. This is a blow to Mr Burnham in his condition, so we are keeping quiet.[6]

It wasn't all bad news. B. M. Joseph scanned the list of survivors and found the name of a friend, Dr Washington Dodge. Joseph wrote his friend a letter, which was mailed when *Olympic* reached Southampton:

On Board RMS *Olympic*, at sea, April 15th.

Dr Washington Dodge.

Dear Sir: I want to congratulate you, Mrs Dodge, and your little child, on your escape from the awful disaster. We, on the sister ship have been rushing to your aid all day, but alas, to no effect. We have positively no news of the disaster, except a partial list of survivors, among whom I was very happy to see your names.

Hoping that your family suffers no ill effects, I remain,

Yours very truly,

B.M. JOSEPH,

With Raphael, Weill & Co.

Los Angeles Herald proprietor Edward Doheny found himself in a position to cover history from the decks of *Olympic*. On Tuesday morning, he filed a story by wireless to Central News Agency:

Frequent bulletins as to the *Titanic* disaster are being posted on the *Olympic*. The latest states that the *Carpathia*, which reached the *Titanic*'s signaled position at daybreak, found only boats and floating wreckage on the surface. All the *Titanic*'s boats have been accounted for, the 675 passengers they contained being mostly women and children. Other steamships are searching in the vicinity for survivors, some of whom have been found.[7]

Doheny wasn't the only newspaperman on board who was filing stories from *Olympic*. Roy W. Howard, general news manager of the United Press, filed a report with his news agency as well:

... *Titanic*'s wireless appeal for help caused tremendous excitement on the *Olympic*, and her passengers and crew are saddened that, despite the fact that the liner raced at full speed all the way, she was unable to be of any assistance to her sister ship.

The *Carpathia* sent the appalling news by wireless, and from that time the *Olympic* constituted herself a relaying station for the smaller vessel.[8]

In his report, filed April 18, Howard said *Olympic*'s passengers were not allowed to send wireless messages until the survivor list and other messages from *Carpathia* were relayed to land stations.

All day Tuesday, the great liner remained practically stationary, flashing the names of the survivors to the land station as fast as she received them from the *Carpathia*. The sympathetic interest of the passengers had to remain unsatisfied until the *Olympic* received instructions to continue her voyage to England. Then the list was published for the benefit of the inquirers, and the embargo on the private use of the ship's wireless instrument was removed.

Titanic's band had played to the last, but *Olympic*'s band was now silent, and would remain so for the rest of the voyage. The music that had lifted the spirits of *Titanic* passengers even at the end might have done the same for those on *Olympic*, and the lack of music added to the sadness that now descended upon the *Olympic*, her passengers and crew.

For *Olympic*'s crew, the grief was overwhelming coming as it did with the burden of survivor's guilt. So many of *Titanic*'s crew had come from *Olympic*, so not only did *Olympic*'s crew know most of those who had died – they were nearly among that tragic group themselves.

As Roy Howard had reported:

The captain's seat in the dining salon, his cabin, everything about the *Olympic* is a reminder of Capt. E. J. Smith, first commander of the *Olympic*, who lost his life on the bridge of the sister ship. There is little talking among the passengers. In hushed whispers, passengers and sailors alike discuss the tragedy which is brought squarely home to everyone here.[9]

Violinist Jock Hume was a promising twenty-nine-year-old, well-known and well-liked when he had served on *Olympic*. His friends now remembered the young man's excitement at the prospect of joining the *Titanic*. Hume was engaged to be married, and he didn't want to miss the chance to be on the new flagship.

Ironically, Hume had been on board *Olympic* last September when she collided with the British cruiser *Hawke*. Hume's mother was unnerved by the incident and begged her son to leave her ocean-going career.[10]

Stewardess Violet Jessop was one of those crew members who transferred from *Olympic* to *Titanic*. She encountered Jock on *Titanic*'s deck shortly after the collision with the iceberg:

As I turned I ran into Jock, the bandleader and his crowd with their instruments. "Funny, they must be going to play," thought I, and at this late hour! Jock smiled in passing, looking rather pale for him, remarking, "Just going to give them a tune to cheer things up a bit," and passed on.[11]

Hume lost his life in the disaster as did all members of *Titanic*'s band, but Jessop survived.

Chief Baker Charles Joughin also found familiar faces when he reported for duty on *Titanic*. 'It was practically a crew from the *Olympic*.'[12]

Titanic's captain personally recruited certain favorites from his *Olympic* crew. He persuaded purser Hugh McElroy and Doctor William Francis Norman O'Loughlin to join him on *Titanic*.

Sixty-two-year-old Dr O'Loughlin grumbled about making a change, but in the end he did as his friend E. J. asked. As his fellow doctor J. C. H. Beaumont recalled:

> Whether he had a premonition about the *Titanic* (I think it is known that [purser] McElroy had) I cannot say, but I do know that during a talk with him in the South Western Hotel he did tell me that he was tired at this time of life to be changing from one ship to another. When he mentioned this to Captain Smith the latter chided him for being lazy and told him to pack up and come with him. So fate decreed 'Billy' should go to the *Titanic* and I to the *Olympic*.

O'Loughlin and McElroy weren't the only members of the crew with misgivings about *Titanic*. Both perished in the sinking.

Gaspare 'Luigi' Gatti had for years served as manager of two Ritz restaurants in London when White Star hired him to join *Olympic* as manager of the à la carte restaurant. Like Hume and Jessop, he was serving on *Olympic* the day the *Hawke* collision occurred. When the chance to transfer to *Titanic* came, Gatti's wife expressed concern:

> She didn't want him to make the trip and said she "felt strange about it." Gatti reassured her, citing *Olympic*'s own brush with disaster last year. "You worry too much," he said. "Didn't I get through the collision aboard the *Olympic* last year without a scratch?"[13]

Gatti joined *Titanic* despite her fears, but her feelings of concern continued.

> On Sunday night, at about the hour when disaster befell the liner, Mrs Gatti had a strange presentiment of danger and throughout the night she was unable to sleep. This feeling had such an effect upon her that the next morning she came to London and remained with a sister. Mr Gatti held a similar position (Restaurant Manager) on the *Olympic* at the time of her collision with the *Hawke*, to that he occupied on the *Titanic*.[14]

Gatti lost his life on *Titanic*.

In picking the top crew for his new command, Captain Smith made a last-minute request that would cause a shuffling of *Titanic*'s officers. He thought it might be a good idea to have *Olympic*'s chief officer, Henry T. Wilde, in the same post on *Titanic*.

Wilde was, after all, familiar with the structure and operation of the new class of vessels. The line agreed, and with Wilde's addition William Murdoch was now demoted to first officer, Charles Lightoller was demoted to second officer, and the former second officer, David Blair, was dropped from the roster altogether. He was assigned to another ship and departed *Titanic* the day before she sailed.

In a postcard to his sister-in-law, Blair wrote: 'This is a magnificent ship, I feel very disappointed I am not to make her first voyage.'

The remaining officers were disappointed as well by their demotions, as Charles Lightoller noted:

> Unfortunately, whilst in Southampton, we had a re-shuffle among the Senior Officers. Owing to the *Olympic* being laid up, the ruling lights of the White Star Line thought it would be a good plan to send the Chief Officer of the *Olympic*, just for the one voyage, as Chief Officer of the *Titanic*, to help, with his experience of her sister ship. This doubtful policy threw both Murdoch and me out of our stride; and, apart from the disappointment of having to step back in our rank, caused quite a little confusion.[15]

Given her previous collision with the *Hawke*, some members of *Olympic*'s crew considered her to be an unlucky ship and were glad to be transferred to the new *Titanic*. Among them was steward George Hickley.[16]

In a letter to his sister on Saturday, April 6, he stated that he passed through Derby on Tuesday (April 2) as he and about a hundred others of the *Olympic* crew went to catch the *Titanic* from Belfast Lough to Southampton. Speaking of the trip, he said they had a fine run down from Belfast, hardly knowing they were on board, and that the *Titanic* seemed a great deal better than the *Olympic*, which he called an unlucky ship.

Hickley, 39, was single. He lost his life in the *Titanic* disaster.

Such examples of loss would weigh heavily on the *Olympic*'s crew, which lacked specifics but knew that much of *Titanic*'s crew was lost.

Moved by the tragedy, *Olympic*'s passengers began collecting money for a *Titanic* Relief Fund. A committee was formed to spearhead the effort, led by some of the wealthier passengers who would also be prime donors. The committee was chaired by New Yorker Albert Wiggin and included Lord Ashburton, Claude Casimir-Perier and the Hon. Cyril Ward.

Wiggin was a good choice on a ship full of bankers and tycoons. In 1904, Wiggin was made the youngest vice president in the history of Chase National Bank. In 1911, he ascended to the bank presidency, from which he oversaw an expansion that would make his bank second only to National City Bank.[17]

New York banker Mortimer Schiff contributed $500 to the relief fund, which would assist survivors and those made widows and orphans by the sinking.[18] By voyage's end, *Olympic*'s passengers had collected about £1,400 for the fund. The money was turned over to Captain Haddock.

Shipboard activity had largely come to a halt on Tuesday, like the ship herself, but much work remained for the ship's Marconi wireless operators.

Olympic had acted as the relay station between *Carpathia* and shore stations for nearly seven hours when, about 10 p.m., the distance between the two ships surpassed the reach of *Olympic*'s wireless equipment. During this time, nearly half of the list of survivors (322 names) had been sent to shore.[19]

By 6.00 a.m. New York time the next morning, *Carpathia* had steamed far enough west to be within range of the wireless station at Sable Island so that the work of relaying the list of survivors could continue.

Her only contribution to the rescue effort now as complete as circumstances would allow, *Olympic* resumed the voyage that had been interrupted nearly 24 hours earlier with her sister ship's desperate pleas for help.

Captain Haddock ordered the ship to resume her course and speed. He steered *Olympic* on a southerly course that would keep her clear of the ice field and the remnants of *Titanic*.

It was a prudent choice, sparing the ship the chance of encountering ice, and sparing her passengers and crew the horrific sights that lingered at the site of *Titanic*'s loss.

Californian's captain had reported Monday afternoon that he found no bodies in the vicinity of the wreck site, but his search had been cursory. Soon, other ships were reporting having seen bodies and wreckage as they steamed through the area.

The sightings were reported to the cable ship *Mackay Bennett*, which departed Halifax, Nova Scotia, just after noon on Wednesday, April 17 on a grim mission. The *Mackay Bennett* had been hired by White Star to retrieve bodies of *Titanic* victims from the North Atlantic. With a cargo hold filled with ice, and a stack of coffins lining her deck, the ship set out for *Titanic*'s last position.

A new day brought little relief to the suffering of *Olympic*'s passengers and crew. By Wednesday *Olympic* was cut off from the *Carpathia* and wireless stations to the west; those who had scanned the survivor lists in search of family and friends were, for the most part, left to wonder and worry. If the names sought weren't on that list of 322 names, the suspense would continue until the ship reached port.

Haddock was once again allowing passengers to send and receive personal wireless messages, but messages were still being censored to ensure no rumors would originate on *Olympic*. In the absence of steady news, however, speculation and rumor were widespread throughout the ship.

One of the most prominent rumors that day had it that the *Californian* had recovered bodies from the wreck site and was taking them to Boston. Roy Howard of United Press passed this on as fact in his next wireless message to New York. When the report reached his office, Philip Franklin questioned the reliability of the source and dismissed the report as a rumor.[20]

Howard's message went on to report:

None save Captain Haddock of the *Olympic*, his wireless operator, the officers of the *Carpathia* and the White Star Line know whether the *Carpathia* told the *Olympic* the full story of the collision and what happened in the dreadful hours while the women and children who were saved along with a few of the men waited, chilled and exhausted, near the spot where the *Titanic* had plunged to her grave.[21]

With *Carpathia* still out to sea, it was difficult to separate fact from fiction. The rescue ship now had all the answers – or as many as the world would likely ever know

– and with her wireless messages devoted almost exclusively to transmitting the list of survivors, newspapers were left to speculate as to the details of the disaster.

The New York Times alone had gotten the story right from the start, and with word that *Carpathia* was due to arrive on Thursday evening, the paper prepared a coverage plan to cover all bases.

The plan included renting an entire floor of a hotel nearest the Cunard pier with phones installed to reach the *Times* copy desk. Sixteen reporters were sent to the pier to cover every conceivable angle, from survivor stories and crowd reactions to hotel accommodations and police arrangements. The biggest 'get' of all was Harold Bride, *Titanic*'s sole surviving wireless operator. His story was sought above all others, and the *Times* intended to get it.

Newspaper editors were desperate for news of *Titanic* and were willing to pay for it. On Wednesday Cape Race related a message from *The World* newspaper to *Olympic* that made the offer plainly:

WIRELESS OFFICER, *Olympic*:
We will pay you liberally for story of rescue of *Titanic*'s passengers any length possible for you to send earliest possible moment. Mention prominent persons. THE WORLD

Olympic's operators didn't dignify the offer with a direct response.

For most of the world, the suspense would end on Thursday, April 18 when *Carpathia* finally arrived in New York. On *Olympic*, however, it was another day of isolation from the news of the world.

Daniel Burnham continued to remain in his stateroom, where he had spent most of *Olympic*'s voyage. He made another entry in his diary:

April 18. Breakfasted alone in the main dining-room. Found a list of subscribers to *Titanic* Relief Fund amounting to £770 or $3,850, headed by Lord Ashburton. Subscribed $100.

To keep herself occupied through the hours of tedium, poet Ella Wheeler Wilcox decided to write a few verses now.

Moved by the thought of so many men having died on *Titanic* so that women and children might live, and by the chivalry and charity she witnessed on *Olympic*, Ella composed a poem she would call 'The Englishman.'

He slams his door in the face of the world
If he thinks the world too bold:
He will even curse; but he opens his purse
To the poor, and the sick, and the old.

He is slow in giving to woman the vote
And slow to pick up her fan;
But he gives her room in an hour of doom
And dies - like an Englishman!

As she would later write of her inspiration, 'It was during this voyage that we, for the first time, realized fully the wonderful power and self-control possessed by the Englishman.'[22]

Captain Smith's widow Eleanor issued a statement that was posted outside White Star offices and would be carried on the front page of the *The Daily Mirror* the next day.

> To My Poor Fellow Sufferers: My heart overflows with grief for you all and is laden with sorrow that you are weighed down with this terrible burden that has been thrust upon us. May God be with us and support us all.
> Yours in deep sympathy,
> Eleanor Smith

While her statement was measured and effective in its thoughtfulness, Eleanor was reportedly delirious in her grief and in denial regarding her husband's terrible fate. It was said that she 'continually mutters, "The *Olympic*'s all right," and seems quite oblivious of the *Titanic*.' It was as if her mind had turned to happier times, when her husband was captain of the *Olympic*.[23]

Captain Haddock had, for this brief period, anyway, been relieved of the pressure of providing information. Philip Franklin had noted as much on Tuesday afternoon when he told reporters that the *Olympic* would soon be out of reach of wireless stations in America and Canada but close enough to provide information to the London office.

Answers soon arrived in the form of the little Cunarder *Carpathia*, which arrived in New York at last about 7 p.m. Thursday. A heavy rain was falling as the ship sailed up the North River and paused alongside the White Star docks. Slowly, *Titanic*'s remaining lifeboats – sixteen in all – were lowered from the rescue ship's decks and towed into piers 58/59.

Then, with *Titanic* survivors lining the decks, *Carpathia* proceeded to her pier, where a crowd of thousands waited to see the event for themselves. At 9.35 p.m., survivors from *Titanic*'s first and second class began to stream out of *Carpathia* into the waiting arms of family and friends. A hush fell over the pier, save for the occasional moan or sob.

Also waiting nearby were aid workers, reporters, photographers and United States Senator William Alden Smith, who had come from Washington to speak with Bruce Ismay. Smith felt the American people were entitled to answers about the circumstances of the disaster, and he intended to see that the US Senate provided them.

Philip Franklin was also on hand to greet Ismay. Together Franklin and Senator Smith boarded *Carpathia*, where they found Ismay still ensconced in the cabin of the ship's doctor. Ismay assured the senator that he and his company would cooperate fully with an American inquiry into the sinking.

The *Times* reporter who was assigned to interview *Titanic*'s junior wireless operator also managed to get on board. Reporters were barred from the ship, but the reporter kept near to wireless inventor Guglielmo Marconi, who also wanted to meet with Harold Bride. Mistaken for Marconi's manager, the reporter was able to reach Bride on board *Carpathia* and the result – another amazing scoop for *The New York Times*.

His story made a thrilling addition to the *Times* coverage of *Carpathia*'s arrival, including his description of *Titanic*'s final moments:

She was a beautiful sight then. Smoke and sparks were rushing out of her funnels. There must have been an explosion, but we heard none. We only saw a big stream of sparks. The ship was gradually turning on her nose - just like a duck does that goes down for a dive. I had only one thing on my mind - to get away from the suction. The band was still playing. I guess all the band went down. They were heroes. They were still playing 'Autumn.'[24]

CHAPTER 10

'So Sad a Landing'

Two days after *Carpathia* reached New York with the survivors of *Titanic*, *Olympic* made her own tragic return to shore.

She carried no survivors – only grieving friends and family of those who, for the most part, had been lost. She wasn't really a hero – although she did help to relay news of the disaster to the rest of the world. She did not reach the *Titanic* in time to be of help – and yet her captain, himself weighed down by considerable grief, felt gratitude for all the help his passengers and crew had been ready to render.

With her flags flying at half-mast, *Olympic* arrived in Plymouth harbor at dawn on April 20 with her passengers and crew still observing a period of mourning that had begun the moment they learned the truth about the *Titanic*. Despite her race toward *Titanic*, *Olympic* was about a day late in reaching port.

As United Press Association General Manager Roy Howard reported when the ship reached Plymouth:

> It was not until the English papers were brought on board that the terrible horror of the *Titanic* disaster was realized by the vessel's company Only the most meagre details were published aboard the ship and as far as possible the officers and Captain Haddock minimized the tragedy enroute because it was feared that the effect would be bad on the ship's company.[1]

Captain Haddock's efforts to minimize the flow of information about the disaster had been effective, but in attempting to minimize the effect of such news, he had created a frenzy when the ship reached port.

'... When the British papers were brought on board here and the great black-faced lists of the dead were read the magnitude of the tragedy came home to all of us. Some of the women passengers on the *Olympic* were on the verge of fainting when they read the names of friends and acquaintances who had gone to the bottom with the great leviathan,' Howard reported.

Reporters who had been waiting for a chance to interview *Olympic* passengers were disappointed to find they knew few details of the disaster itself and were more interested in reading the news than becoming part of it.

First Class passenger E. Marshall Fox, European representative for the US Steel Corporation, expressed his relief that the ship had finally reached port.

'We are thankful that the voyage is over,' Fox said. 'The suspense and anxiety were terrible, and then the knowledge that so many men, women and children were lost is frightful. The passengers and crew were struck dumb by the enormity of the disaster. When word was passed around it probably would be necessary for *Olympic*'s passengers to make room for the rescued, all hands displayed eagerness to do everything possible.'

Like her fellow passengers, Ella Wheeler Wilcox was stunned by the headlines. 'Only on the arrival of the *Olympic* at the English port was the whole awful truth revealed to us. It was a dramatic hour never to be forgotten.'[2]

Wilcox shared the poem she had been inspired to write during the voyage with a British newspaper, which published it.

Soon newspapers on both sides of the Atlantic were sharing *Olympic*'s story with *Titanic*-obsessed readers.

> It was early at luncheon time on Monday that news of the disaster, which at first was kept secret, was made known to the passengers. Every one broke into tears, and since then not a smile has been seen on any face. The orchestra no longer played, and the voyage, which had begun gayly, ended in mourning. Among the crew the deepest sadness prevails.

In speaking to *Olympic*'s crew, reporters detected a tension that had developed during the past four days on board ship.

> All sorts of rumors were current and it was even stated that the *Olympic*'s crew would refuse to accompany her on the next trip unless steps were taken to remedy this on the voyage.

The ship's crew, it seemed, felt a 'dissatisfaction with the life-saving arrangements' on board *Olympic* as on *Titanic*.

They were not alone.

Once the world got word of *Titanic*'s critical lifeboat shortage – and the resulting loss of life – there was a public outcry. Every steamship company under the stewardship of the British Board of Trade would be affected. Lifeboat regulations ratified by the board in 1894, which applied to ships up to 10,000 gross tons, meant most ships above 10,000 gross tons, including the 46,000 ton *Titanic*, failed to carry enough lifeboats for all aboard, which after the *Titanic*'s loss had become the new standard. Cunard's *Mauretania*, for instance, could carry 2,972 people but had enough seats in her lifeboats for only 962.

Editorial cartoons and editorials in papers on both sides of the Atlantic carried the battle cry, 'Boats for all.'

Olympic's passengers had their own grievances.

> It is evident that the news of the disaster was withheld for many hours from relatives and friends of those who were drowned. The *Olympic*'s passengers are emphatic to expressing hope that those responsible for with-holding the news of the tragedy for a whole day should be exposed and if possible made to suffer for their strange conduct.

As the ship was at anchor in Plymouth, a heavy mist descended upon the English Channel. The change in weather fit the solemn mood on board ship perfectly, but it would delay *Olympic* in getting to Cherbourg.

Exhausted after the long vigil for *Titanic* and shattered by news of the disaster, Captain Haddock was reluctant to speak to reporters about the events of April 14–15 when reporters put questions to him.

The press, however, couldn't be avoided so easily. Starting with its scoop on the night of April 14, *The New York Times* continued to cover the *Titanic* story masterfully and seemed to have reporters everywhere. Reporter W. Orton Tewson began collecting stories from the ship's passengers and crew.

His stories, filed from Plymouth, Cherbourg and Southampton, would give the world the first taste of what life had been like on the sister ship since hearing *Titanic*'s calls for help.

The appetite for *Titanic* news remained insatiable, in fact, from the moment fragmentary reports had first emerged on Monday morning. And while the world had been devouring the stories for days, only now did the man who had first conceived of the *Olympic* and *Titanic* learn that his latest, greatest achievement was gone.

Lord Pirrie had undergone an operation in early spring to relieve the pain associated with a swollen prostate and was now recovering aboard his yacht, *Valiant*, in the Baltic Sea. His poor health had prevented him from making *Titanic*'s maiden voyage. When word reached the yacht of *Titanic*'s sinking, Pirrie's wife, Margaret, actively kept the news from her ailing husband until the last possible moment.

By April 20, *Valiant*, like the *Olympic*, was nearing England. Margaret knew she would have to tell her husband what had happened. Taking a seat at her husband's bedside, she broke the awful news. *Titanic* had struck an iceberg and sank in less than three hours. Hundreds of people were lost, including his nephew, Thomas Andrews, along with the entire guarantee group from Harland & Wolff. Bruce Ismay had survived and was now being questioned in America as part of an official investigation into the disaster.

Though immobilized by illness, the news stirred the master shipbuilder. 'Pirrie bucked against his pillows as though he had been shot. He lay without speaking in his dimly lit stateroom for what seemed like an hour, finally asking Margaret for his lap desk.'[3]

Once the initial shock of the tragedy passed, the shipbuilder dispatched an order by wireless to Edward Wilding, naval architect at Harland & Wolff: 'Find out what happened to that ship. Pirrie.'

At 1.30 p.m. Saturday, *Olympic* entered Cherbourg waters, an hour later than expected. Her sister ship had also been an hour late 10 days ago on what would be her only arrival and departure from this harbor. The mood, however, was entirely different, as *The New York Herald* reported:

> Never has the harbor of Cherbourg seen so sad a landing as that of the passengers of the *Olympic*.[4]

Here again there was a rush for newspapers, this time the European edition of the *Herald* being in great demand, as the ship's company continued to seek the latest news and, for the first time, many passengers have learned of *Olympic*'s lifeboat shortage.

The *Herald* correspondent heard the seeds of discontent when talking with *Olympic*'s passengers and crew, noting that:

> Many passengers and sailors expressed their dissatisfaction at the life saving arrangements. All sorts of rumors were current and it was even stated that the *Olympic*'s crew would refuse to accompany her on the next trip unless steps were taken to remedy this on the voyage.

An *Olympic* passenger who did talk to reporters was R. H. Benson, and in doing so he demonstrated that where few facts existed, *Olympic*'s passengers had filled in the blanks with rumors and speculation.

Describing the early distress calls, Benson said:

> The message added that the passengers already had taken to the boats; also that two ships were standing by. We were told that we were to take over the *Baltic*'s mail for England and that the *Baltic* would return to New York with the *Titanic*'s passengers. It was also stated that the *Carpathia* and another vessel in addition to the *Baltic* were cruising around the scene, but this was not borne out by what we have read since reaching Plymouth.

Olympic's passengers had undoubtedly suffered in the days since *Titanic* sank, but they had been spared the worst of it. The details of the disaster had been kept from them and their ship had steered clear of the horrors to be found in the area surrounding *Titanic*'s final position.

Two steamers – the *Rhein* and the *Bremen* – weren't so lucky. Each passed through *Titanic*'s top-side grave on April 20 and reported seeing 'a great number of human bodies with life preservers on floating in the sea.'[5]

In all, *Bremen*'s officers estimated they had seen more than 100 bodies along with wreckage that included an overturned lifeboat, steamer chairs and small fragments of wood.

Bremen's officers declined to offer more details, but Johanna Stunke, a first class passenger on *Bremen*, provided a vivid description of what she and other passengers had seen from *Bremen*'s deck:[6]

> It was between 4 and 5 o'clock, Saturday, April 20th, when our ship sighted an iceberg off the bow to the starboard. As we drew nearer, and could make out small dots floating around in the sea, a feeling of awe and sadness crept over everyone on the ship.
>
> We passed within a hundred feet of the southernmost drift of the wreckage, and looking down over the rail we distinctly saw a number of bodies so clearly that we could make out what they were wearing and whether they were men or women.
>
> We saw one woman in her night dress, with a baby clasped closely to her breast. Several women passengers screamed and left the rail in a fainting condition. There was another woman, fully dressed, with her arms tight around the body of a shaggy dog.
>
> The bodies of three men in a group, all clinging to one steamship chair, floated near by, and just beyond them were a dozen bodies of men, all of them encased in life-

preservers, clinging together as though in a last desperate struggle for life. We couldn't see, but imagined that under them was some bit of wreckage to which they all clung when the ship went down, and which didn't have buoyancy enough to support them.

Those were the only bodies we passed near enough to distinguish, but we could see the white life-preservers of many more dotting the sea, all the way to the iceberg. The officers told us that was probably the berg hit by the *Titanic*, and that the bodies and ice had drifted along together.

Mrs Stunke said a number of the passengers demanded that the *Bremen* stop and pick up the bodies, but the officers assured them that they had just received a wireless message saying the cable ship *Mackay-Bennett* was only two hours away from the spot, and was coming for that express purpose.

Bremen passed word of the bodies to *Mackay-Bennett*, along with the approximate position. In the vicinity *Bremen* saw an iceberg that matched the description of the one *Titanic* had struck. Smaller bergs were sighted the same day, but at some distance from where the *Titanic* sank.

At Cherbourg, the Burnhams departed *Olympic* with heavy hearts. The couple travelled to their accommodations at the city's Grand Hotel Du Casino, where Daniel Burnham tried to express his feelings the next day in a letter of sympathy to Francis Millet's widow:[7]

> Dear Lilly,
> They tell me today that there is little hope. I cannot believe it. The world will be empty without Frank. He has meant more to me than I imagined while I had him, although I knew well how very dear he was to me. The love and the wisdom he had had has been unfailing and the hard and constant struggles of many years have been lightened by his sure, steady care. I have always pointed him out to my sons as a man to match and imitate; he has taught me and them to serve others, and do it with unselfishness. To serve! this is to be a man, and who else equalled him. I am glad that the time before me is short and that I am not to live long without him. We expect to be in England about a month from now when I want very much to see you ...
> In deep love and sorrow,
> D. H. Burnham

Olympic was soon steaming away from Cherbourg for her next port, Southampton. Reporter W. Orton Tewson, along with reporter H. Leatherdale of *The London Daily Express*, who was also now reporting from *Olympic*'s decks, wrote a message to Captain Haddock about the 'All *Titanic* passengers safe' wireless message, which, they pointed out, had caused a drop in *Titanic*'s re-insurance on April 15 from 60 to 20 guineas. The pressing question was, if Haddock had 'ever received such a message, and if so, if [he] knew whence it came?'

Captain Haddock's reluctance to discuss the *Titanic* disaster came not only from his own reticence when it came to publicity, but also from his lack of information about the drama for which he had been a participant.

But the question dealt with one thing he could speak to – what messages his ship had received and sent – so he drafted a statement to share with Tewson and Leatherdale. Assuring the two that *Olympic* sent no such message, he asked the ship's wireless operators to verify the same. When Moore and Bagot did so, Haddock showed the reporters his statement, which had already been sent to Bruce Ismay.

> On the passage from Cherbourg I received the inclosed letter from H. Leatherdale of *The London Daily Express*, to whom and also to W. Orton Tewson of *The New York Times*, in the presence of our Marconi operators, I have diened [*sic*] that such a message was received or sent from Capt. Haddock.

It was from a lady resident in New York, a constant White Star traveler, whose name is that of a well-known Canadian steamship line. The exact text was:

> Received from Sable Island, 10:20 M., east (3:30 p.m. Greenwich time.) – Commander Haddock, *Olympic* – Are all *Titanic* passengers safe?

The remaining part of the inaccurate message, Capt. Haddock's letter to his owners stated, was probably suggested by the following wireless from the steamship *Asian*, telling of the last pathetic calls from the *Titanic* before her power gave out:

> Received 8:35 a.m. Monday, New York time (1:31 p.m. Greenwich).
> *Asian* heard MGY (the *Titanic*) signaling on and off from 8 to 10 p.m., local time, Sunday. Messages too faint to read. Finished calling S.O.S. at midnight. Position given as latitude 41.46, longitude 50.14. No further information. *Asian* then three hundred miles west of *Titanic* and towing oil tanks to *Halifax*. Regards, WOOD.

As a report in *The New York Times* would note:

> The inference drawn by Capt. Haddock is that some unknown persons tapped these two messages, missing part of them, and evolved the misleading message to the effect that all the *Titanic* passengers were safe and she was towing to Halifax, which they had stolen in mid-air, the second message relating to the *Titanic*.

Haddock's statement continued with an admission that he had also jumbled the first message but had not transmitted it to other stations:

> I on receipt of the first message made the same mistake and left out the "are." I telephoned this to the inquiry office on the *Olympic* to post a notice reading, "All *Titanic* passengers safe." Nothing more was added.
> We have been most carefully through every message from the ship. No copy of my error, plain or code, or remainder of the sentence was sent from this ship.
> I am showing this letter to Messrs Leatherdale and Tewson.
> H. J. Haddock, Commander.

After the reporters had read the statement, which would soon be in papers worldwide, Haddock concluded: 'That is the only light I can throw on the mystery of those unofficial messages sent out.'

As he told the reporters: 'The story that I sent the report about the *Virginian* towing the *Titanic* is a flagrant invention,' he said. 'So soon as I heard of the disaster from the *Carpathia* I dispatched the news by wireless to New York, informing White Star officials of the number of persons saved and of the foundering of the *Titanic*. That was on Monday afternoon. The *Olympic* steamed nearly 400 miles before discovering that she would be too late to render any aid.'

While the ship was still en route to Southampton, Haddock filled out a confidential report to the Marconi Company, dated April 20, 1912, in which he praised the ship's wireless operators for their performance over the past few days.

'The following is a report on Mr E. Moore and A. Bagot.' Haddock rated the operators together with a 'VG' for Very Good in all categories, which included Attention to Duties, General Conduct, Personal Appearance and Sobriety. Under remarks he wrote: 'Can scarcely speak too highly of these officers' conduct at a very trying & anxious time. Mr Moore especially worthy of promotion. Thoughtful & reliable. (Signed) H. J. Haddock, Commander.'

Olympic departed the French port later that afternoon and continued the last leg of her journey to England. She arrived in Southampton Dock at about 2 a.m. on Sunday, April 21. It was another sad arrival – her third in two days – but Southampton was saddest of all.

It was from this port that *Titanic* had sailed, and the city was hit hardest by the horrific losses suffered among *Titanic*'s crew.

Olympic arrived at the same pier where her sister had departed a mere eleven days earlier. Her passengers, most clad in the black clothes of formal mourning, disembarked. Captain Haddock summoned his exhausted wireless operators to his cabin to offer his thanks for all that they had done since Sunday night.

Haddock himself was so exhausted that he slept through the remainder of the morning.

On board ship, however, work began immediately for *Olympic*'s turn-around. Despite her fourteen-hour race at top speed toward *Titanic*, she had been stationary for most of the 16th and was a day late, reaching port on the 21st.

She was scheduled to depart again on the Wednesday, April 24, giving her crew just three days to prepare the liner for the voyage. The timeline for turning the big ship around had always been strenuous, but this time the company had the added responsibility of adding additional lifeboats to the upper deck, as *The New York Times* reported:

Ceaseless efforts are being made at Southampton to put enough boats aboard the *Olympic* before her sailing on Wednesday. It is absolutely essential that this be done, for otherwise, it is understood, the passengers and crew insist that the sailing be postponed.

It has not been possible to get the necessary number of solid lifeboats in time, but thirty-five additional collapsible boats arrived aboard this afternoon, and five more are expected. The boat deck will be almost entirely filled with boats. A thorough testing of all the life-saving appliances, and, possibly, an elaborate boat drill will be held before the *Olympic* sails again.

The *Olympic* will take aboard at New York the lifeboats of the *Titanic*, which are now there.[8]

As crews worked to place all of the new collapsible boats to the Boat Deck, Haddock granted *The Daily Mail*'s special correspondent's request for an interview.[9]

Having had time to read the newspapers and catch up on what the world had known for nearly a week, Haddock was able to clarify some of the statements he'd made earlier and share his thoughts on the disaster.

He was greatly surprised, he said, to learn that the loss of the *Titanic* was caused by an iceberg. 'A week before the *Titanic* sunk the *Olympic* passed over the very spot, or a few miles north of it, in broad daylight,' he said. 'We never saw a single particle of ice of any description, and from the bridge of the *Olympic* we could see, I should think, twenty miles on either side.'

Of course, on the return journey he took a more southerly course to avoid the ice field that had doomed the sister ship. Haddock estimated that his ship had reached a speed of 23 to 24 knots in her attempt to be of assistance.

Haddock repeated his statement regarding the confusing 'All Saved from *Titanic*' message, this time elaborating on the messages that he believed had been misunderstood to form it.

The message that came from one of our old passengers, a lady in New York, and it was "Are all the *Titanic* passengers saved?" The lady had friends in the *Titanic*, and she was anxious about them. That message was received on Monday at about 10:20 or 10:27 a.m., New York time.

On Monday, White Star got a reminder that the race for domination of the North Atlantic shipping lanes would go on.

The French Line's new 23,000 ton, 713-foot *France* departed Havre on her maiden voyage to New York. The *France* had the misfortune of echoing the *Titanic* story – the world's newest ship on her maiden voyage to New York – as the horrors of the worst disaster in maritime history still dominated the headlines – and imaginations – of the world.

As a precaution aimed at calming passenger concerns, the line sent *La Touraine* on the same route just after *France*'s departure to act as an escort and stand-by rescue ship should disaster strike.[10]

On the same day, White Star announced two post-*Titanic* developments:

It is understood that the plans of the White Star liner *Gigantic*, which is now being built in Belfast and which was to have been 1,000 feet in length, will be modified. It is probable that the new plans will provide for double cellular bottom and sides, such as the *Mauretania* and *Lusitania* have, as a stipulated condition of receiving the government subsidy.[11]

Gigantic was the third of the *Olympic* class liners. White Star was so pleased with the early success of *Olympic* that before *Titanic* was even launched, the company had ordered this third ship.[12]

> *Gigantic* to be Biggest Liner
> Queenstown, Nov. 24, 1911 – It is stated here that the proposed new thousand foot steamship to be built for the White Star line will be provided, among other things, with golf links and a cricket court. She is to be named the *Gigantic*.

Her keel had been laid on Nov. 30, 1911 in the same slip under the Arrol Gantry where *Olympic* had been built. With the loss of *Titanic*, work on *Gigantic* stopped while the team at Harland & Wolff consulted with White Star about changes that would obviously need to be made.

The builders wouldn't have the benefit of Thomas Andrews' notes from *Titanic's* maiden voyage, but the improvements needed were, for the most part, self-evident.

First, the name. Perhaps it was no longer a good idea to associate these new liners with gods or mythical beings of substantial size. From the moment her keel was laid, the ship had been called *Gigantic* in press reports – and in shipyard documents. But now, with *Titanic* gone, White Star went into action to free their new ship, not yet launched, from associations with the disaster.

On May 31, 1912, ironically the first anniversary of *Titanic's* launch, the line went public with *Gigantic's* new name:[13]

> Considered a lucky name
> White Star Liner to Take Place of the *Titanic* to be Called *Britannic*.

> New York, May 31 - It is announced here that the new 50,000 ton White Star liner which will take the place of the *Titanic* in the fall of 1913 is to be named *Britannic*. It will be the same length as the *Olympic*, 869 feet. The White Star line has had two vessels bearing the name *Britannic*. They both earned large sums for the company and the name is considered lucky.

White Star would await the results of two official inquiries into the *Titanic* disaster – one in America, the other in Great Britain – before making any final decisions about design changes for *Britannic*. It would also need to make such changes to *Olympic*, but for now she was needed in service.

Olympic would have to make do with whatever quick fixes White Star could put in place – which amounted to additional collapsible lifeboats and a change in course to follow a more southerly route on westbound crossings.

The same day that White Star announced that design changes were likely for *Gigantic*, the line also announced that the *Olympic* has been provided with forty collapsible boats. For the next crossing, however, she would only carry twenty-four collapsible boats, which, when added to the ship's standard complement of lifeboats, put the ship in compliance with the new 'boats for all' edict with sixteen wooden lifeboats under davits supplemented by a total of twenty-eight collapsible boats.

CHAPTER 11
The Aftermath

The White Star Line tried to pick up the pieces after the shattering news of *Titanic*'s loss, but the company faced challenges on several fronts in the days and weeks after the disaster.

The company itself was under the magnifying glass of the United States Senate as the *Titanic* inquiry led by Sen. William Alden Smith, Republican from Michigan, got underway at the Waldorf Astoria hotel in New York City. (The British would conduct their own inquiry following the American inquiry).

The first witness was Bruce Ismay, followed by eighty-five others in eighteen days of testimony. The final transcript, when finished, was more than 1,000 pages long.

White Star's attentions were divided between the inquiry, at which key personnel including Ismay, Philip Franklin, Captain Haddock and others would be called to testify. A large portion of *Titanic*'s surviving crew was also being held over in case the inquiry should need their testimony.

Ismay alone was a public relations nightmare on an epic scale. The American press was calling him a coward or worse. One headline, THAYER DIED HERO UNLIKE LIVING ISMAY, said what all articles suggested – that Ismay had no right to be alive when so many people had died on his ship.

With a shortage of personnel, White Star struggled to maintain a sailing schedule that was now without one of its biggest players. Additionally, there was the colossal task of adding lifeboats to the remaining ships and expediting their next sailings.

To achieve continuous service, White Star needed every ship it had. Just three days after her return from her harrowing experiences in mid-ocean, *Olympic* stood ready for another crossing on the morning of April 24.

With 1,400 passengers on board, the ship was just twenty minutes from departing when several firemen announced that the collapsible boats that had been hastily added to the ship were unseaworthy. The men sent a request to White Star's Southampton manager, Mr Curry, asking that the collapsible boats be replaced with wooden lifeboats. It was impossible, Curry said, to do so right now – and by way of assurance told the men that the British Board of Trade had inspected the boats and found them to be seaworthy.

This answer did not satisfy the complaints, and the ship's firemen, greasers and trimmers – 276 men in all – stopped working and left the ship.

As one *Olympic* fireman explained to a sympathetic passenger:

Can you imagine what it is like? We were cooped together in the bows of the ship when we heard what had happened to the *Titanic*. We put on full speed and came close to the place where she sank. That set us men talking. Some of us had friends on that ship. Here are we, close to the water-line, in the bows. If there is a collision, what happens? We are smashed to atoms; we haven't a chance. Or if there is a wreck, and the boats are put out, who suffers if there are not enough boats? The firemen. The passengers are saved first, and some of the seamen man the boats. But if we are short of boats, the fireman is certain of drowing.[1]

Mr Curry advised Captain Haddock that the action constituted mutiny and that the master could, at his discretion, have the men placed aboard the ship.

The striking crew members met at the dock to talk with the secretary of the Seafarers' Union, who told the men he would he abide by their decision. The men voted unanimously to strike.

Olympic sailed as far as Spithead without the strikers before stopping to await a resolution to the problem. White Star hired a new crew to replace the strikers, which caused new trouble. Soon a group of sailors departed the ship, stating that they would not sail on a ship with the new non-union crew. Captain Haddock signaled a nearby ship and asked that the men be taken ashore and charged with mutiny.[2]

For a time it was thought that *Olympic* might sail the next day, but the issue proved too complicated – especially given nerves of the ship's crew made raw by the recent loss of so many of their friends on the *Titanic*.

A group of *Olympic's* passengers – seventy-two in all – volunteered to work in the stokehold, and the Duke of Sutherland offered to raise a crew of yachtsmen.

Ralph Sweet, one of the first class passengers who volunteered to serve as a stoker said:

Our idea was that we should stoke the boat to Queenstown, where the Captain would have been able to get fresh men. About a hundred passengers volunteered altogether, and we would have been able to work in short watches. Capt. Haddock thanked us very nicely, and I thought he was going to put us to work right away, but he told us afterward that he would not call on our services.

It was a terrible blow so soon after *Titanic's* loss, but White Star decided to cancel the voyage completely.

Captain Haddock's handling of the situation had impressed the Duke of Sutherland, who said:

I think all the passengers will be sorry that they are not sailing under Capt. Haddock's care. As for the complaint that he did not give the passengers sufficient information, I do not know what more he could have given them. Certainly he told them everything he knew. He got the firemen, and I have no doubt that if he had had more time he would have got the rest of the crew together.

Olympic returned to Southampton, where she would remain until May 15. On that date, exactly a month after *Titanic* sank, *Olympic* sailed out of Southampton on her first voyage since the disaster with slightly more than 400 passengers – the lowest number of her career.

When she reached New York, she was visited by Sen. William Alden Smith, who thought it would be helpful to his inquiry to see the inner workings of *Titanic*'s sister ship. Lord Mersey, who oversaw the British inquiry into the *Titanic*, had already been given his own tour of *Olympic* on May 6 while the ship was idle in Southampton.

While Senator Smith was on board ship, he spoke with Captain Haddock and Senior Wireless Operator Ernest Moore, who gave him a copy of the ship's wireless log covering the hours relating to the *Titanic* disaster.

Haddock provided the senator and his group with a tour, which included testing a lifeboat, which was lowered down *Olympic*'s side fully loaded with sailors.

Haddock mentioned that Frederick Barrett, leading fireman on *Titanic*, was on board. He then led Smith to the boiler room, where Barrett described for the senator and his party what had happened on board *Titanic* in the aftermath of the collision with the iceberg.

On the return voyage *Olympic* nearly had a collision of her own – with the rocky cliffs of Land's End at the tip of England. The ship was running at high speed at 10 p.m. on June 1 when a lookout spotted breaking water at the base of the rocks. The ship's engines were ordered 'Full astern' and she narrowly avoided running aground. The incident was kept quiet at the time – so near to the loss of the *Titanic*. The near-collision was the result of a navigational error that had put her miles off course, and Captain Haddock was forced to submit to the humiliation of having a monitor on the bridge for future voyages.[3]

Ongoing fascination with the *Titanic* disaster probably helped the *Olympic*'s cause as much as it hurt. For every passenger who avoided her out of fear, another would be curious to see the sister ship up close and explore the locations made famous by the sinking, from the boat deck itself, where most of the drama had played out, to the gymnasium, where Colonel Astor had cut open his lifebelt to show his young bride, Madeleine, what was inside.

One *Titanic* survivor even got into the act. During one of her stays in New York, Col Archibald Gracie visited *Olympic* to refresh his memory of *Titanic* locales as he did research for his book, *The Truth about the Titanic*.[4]

I recently visited the sister ship of the *Titanic*, viz., the *Olympic*, at her dock in New York harbor. This was for the purpose of still further familiarizing myself with the corresponding localities which were the scene of my personal experiences on the *Titanic*, and which are referred to in this narrative. The only difference in the deck plan of the sister ship which I noted, and which the courteous officers of the *Olympic* mentioned, is the latter ship's Deck A is not glass-enclosed like the *Titanic*'s; but one of the principal points that I made during my investigation concerns the matter of the alleged breaking in two of this magnificent ship. The White Star Line officers pointed out to me what they called the ship's "forward expansion joint," and they claimed the *Titanic* was so constructed that she must have split in two at this point, if she did so at all. I was interested in observing that this "expansion joint" was less than twelve feet forward from that point on the Boat Deck whence I jumped, as described (to the iron railing on the roof of the officers' quarters).

Col Gracie died on December 4, 1912, but he had completed his book on the *Titanic* disaster, which was published posthumously. While the official cause of death was complications from diabetes, Gracie's family felt that he had died as a result of the cold night he spent on an overturned collapsible after pulling himself out of the freezing waters of the North Atlantic.

Olympic's bookings increased somewhat that summer, but she again hit hard times while departing New York on July 6. Just as she approached the Statue of Liberty, the ship's steering malfunctioned. *Olympic* was not under control, and Captain Haddock warned other ships in the harbor of this as the ship came to a stop, her bow nudged into the mud.

It was an image of which White Star's nightmares were made – *Titanic*'s sister ship run aground at the edge of New York harbor in full view of thousands of people along the shore, with Lady Liberty looking on as if disapprovingly.

Repairs were handled quickly, and within an hour Haddock steamed out of New York harbor and out to sea. While some articles quoted unnamed marine experts who praised Captain Haddock's handling of the incident, other papers showed a clear bias against White Star in their coverage of the incident:

LINER *OLYMPIC* IS RACING OVER SEA AFTER ACCIDENT

After plunging heavily into a mud flat off the Jersey coast at Communipaw, the huge White Star liner *Olympic* – sister ship of the *Titanic* – refloated after an hour's straining effort, turned to her course and sped away across the Atlantic.

That the *Olympic* sustained some injury to her hull that may develop into serious trouble in midocean was feared by shipping men and by the thousands who witnessed the accident from harbor craft from the Jersey shore and from Ellis Island.

The giant ocean greyhouse was no sooner hauled off the treacherous shoal by a float of tugs than clouds of smoke belched from her lofty funnels, a great wave of foam was tossed at the stern by her propellers, and true to the tradition of her owners she raced away to make up for lost time – speed at any cost.[5]

Olympic's future, like the ship herself, seemed stuck in the mud. With the American and British investigations into the *Titanic* disaster now concluded, it was time for White Star to act on the official recommendations to make the ship safer and, if possible, restore the travelling public's faith in the line itself. In mid-August the company announced that the *Olympic* would be withdrawn from service in November to effect changes to the ship.

During the coming winter the White Star Steamship *Olympic* will undergo a renovation costing close to £200,000. The principal alteration will be the provision of side bunkers which practically means an inner or second shell.

The decision of the White Star Line to renovate the *Olympic* is in accordance with a recommendation given in the judgment pronounced by the British Board of Trade inquiry into the *Titanic* disaster, that sea going ships in addition to their water tight transverse bulkheads be provided with a double skin carried above the water line or with a longitudinal vertical water tight bulkhead on each side of the vessel or both.[6]

Olympic's withdrawal from service came sooner than expected, however, when she lost another propeller blade at 12.45 a.m. on Friday, September 13.

> Many second-class passengers hurried on deck, fearing that a collision had occurred, so great was the vibration when the blade of the propeller dropped off, but they were quickly assured, and returned to their cabins.
>
>   The first class passengers, further away from the stern, did not feel the vibration to any serious extent, and most of them continued their slumber without disturbance. They heard of the accident at breakfast time.[7]

The ship made one more round-trip from Southampton, starting on September 18, before she was removed from service and sent to Belfast for her post-*Titanic* refit, which would not be completed until March 1913.

The primary purpose of the refit was to enact the recommendations of the *Titanic* inquiries in order to make *Olympic* impervious to the damage that had doomed her sister ship. This included a double skin and changes to her watertight bulkheads, five of which now extended as high as B-Deck, and the addition of a sixteenth bulkhead. The changes meant *Olympic* could, in theory, survive with six of the first watertight compartments flooded (as opposed to the original four on the original *Olympic* and *Titanic*).

Safety was the primary reason for change, but Harland & Wolff also used this time to incorporate other lessons from *Titanic* into *Olympic*'s design. By the time they were finished, *Titanic* and *Olympic* were closer to twins than ever before. The Marconi room where Moore and Bagot had toiled so hard through the events of April 14–15 was relocated to the center of the officers' quarters. The Reading and Writing Room was reduced in size, as it had been on *Titanic*, to make room for more first class staterooms. The Café Parisian that have proven so popular among the younger set on *Titanic* was added to *Olympic* as well, giving B Deck a welcoming space that mimicked a French sidewalk café.

Also like *Titanic*, *Olympic*'s first class reception room adjacent to the Dining Saloon was extended to accommodate more passengers who wished to lounge at the base of the aft Grand Staircase.

Lessons may have been learned in the redesign of watertight bulkheads and double skins, but claims of unsinkability were once again being applied to *Olympic* – now 'two ships in one' – when the press described the refitted ship.

> The 45,000-ton *Olympic*, which still has the distinction of being the largest steamship afloat, left today for Southampton to get ready to sail for New York a week from Wednesday. For nearly four months the giant vessel had been in drydock at Harland & Wolff's shipyard, undergoing alterations designed to make her the "safest" ship in the world. At an expense of $1,500,000 the vessel has been fitted with an inner hull to make her, as far as engineering skill can, unsinkable. The original double bottom of the ship has been extended upward to a point well above the water line,

thus furnishing an interior skin or solid steel and forming a hull within a hull so that the *Olympic* is now described as "two ships in one." In the opinion of engineering experts the *Olympic* could now pass safely through such an accident that befell her sister ship, the ill-fated *Titanic*, since the effect of running on a sunken reef or submerged iceberg would be merely to rip the outer hull.[8]

Ready to take her place again in the North Atlantic run, *Olympic* departed Belfast on March 22 for Southampton and the resumption of her career.

On Wednesday, April 2, *Olympic* left her Southampton berth and steamed into the harbor where she 'was greeted with a roar of salutes from the whistles of all the craft in the harbor as she left her dock and moved majestically out into the channel.'[9]

On April 13, 1913, one day before the first anniversary of *Titanic*'s sinking, *Olympic* arrived in New York harbor for the first time in her new skin.

White Star faced the question of safety head on, and in papers across the United States, a statement from 'the builders' reassured the public that *Olympic* could not, by design, suffer the same fate as her sister.

> The builders insist that no such disaster as befell the *Titanic* could befall the *Olympic* for the reason that collision with an iceberg would not destroy her. If struck a glancing blow the inner shell would keep her afloat long enough to allow all to be saved.[10]

Olympic was now 'two ships in one' with lifeboats for all, but it had taken the *Titanic* disaster to force the changes. Voices that had called for changes before the sinking had been ignored. One such voice, according to a friend who later spoke with the press, belonged to Captain Smith himself.

Magazine writer Glenn Marston had been a passenger on Smith's last westward voyage as *Olympic*'s captain. During the crossing the two men had a conversation that must surely rank as one of the most interesting – and foreboding – of any ever to take place on the high seas.[11]

Marston remarked to Captain Smith that the *Olympic* appeared to be carrying a small number of lifeboats given the number of people on board, to which Smith replied:

> If the ship was to strike a submerged derelict or iceberg that would cut through into several of the water-tight compartments we have not enough boats or rafts aboard to take care of more than one-third of the passengers.

According to Marston, the captain said the same was true of the new *Titanic*, of which he would be taking command when *Olympic* returned to England.

As Captain Smith put it:

> The *Titanic*, too, is no better equipped. It ought to carry at least double the number of boats and rafts it does to afford any real protection to the passengers. Besides, there is always danger of some of the boats becoming damaged or swept away before they can be manned.

Smith told his friend that when he visited Belfast during *Titanic*'s construction he 'noticed the small number of life-saving devices and was not satisfied.' But, as Marston recalled, 'He was also unable to induce the company officials to equip the *Titanic* with additional boats and rafts when he took command of that ship.'

Marston asked his friend why the White Star Line would take such a chance. Was it the money?

'No,' Smith replied.

> I don't think it's from motives of economy as the additional equipment would cost only a trifle when compared to the cost of the ship, but the builders nowadays believe that their boats are practically indestructable, as far as sinking goes, because of the water-tight bulkheads, and that the only need of lifeboats at all is for purposes of rescue from other ships that are not so modernly constructed or to land passengers in case the ship goes ashore. They hardly regard them as life-saving equipment.

Smith went further.

> Personally, I believe that a ship ought to carry enough boats and rafts to carry every soul aboard it. I have followed the sea now for forty years and have attributed my success in not having an accident, until we were rammed by the *Hawke* in the Solent in Southampton, and I was exonerated in that case, to never taking a chance.
>
> I always take the safe course. While there is only one chance in a thousand that a ship like the *Olympic* or *Titanic* may meet with an accident that would injure it so severely that it would sink before aid would arrive, yet if I had my way both ships would be equipped with twice the number of lifeboats and rafts. In the old days it was different from today with the mergers and the trusts in the steamship business. Now the captain has little to say regarding equipment. All of that has been taken out of his hands and is taken care of at the main office.

Tragically for Smith and a lot of other people, one chance in a thousand came to pass on April 14, 1912, and in the seconds it took for ice to damage steel, all the best laid plans for *Olympic* and *Titanic* came to a sudden, devastating end. The twin sisters Pirrie and Ismay had first imagined years before as the dominant forces on the North Atlantic were parted only days after their partnership on the North Atlantic had begun.

For the *Olympic*, her owners and crew, things would never be quite the same again.

Perhaps *Titanic* survivor Jack Thayer said it best.

> There was peace, and the world had an even tenor to its way. Nothing was revealed in the morning the trend of which was not known the night before. It seems to me that the disaster about to occur was the event that not only made the world rub its eyes and awake but woke it with a start, keeping it moving at a rapidly accelerating pace ever since with less and less peace, satisfaction and happiness. To my mind the world of today awoke April 15th, 1912.[12]

CHAPTER 12

Epilogue

Many lives intersected through the events of April 14–15, 1912. Some people emerged as heroes, while others were labeled cowards. Most were haunted by the 'what ifs' of the *Olympic-Titanic* story.

- What if *Olympic* hadn't suffered a collision with the *Hawke*, which caused a delay in finishing *Titanic*?
- What if *Olympic* had been more seriously damaged by *Hawke*, perhaps causing a redesign?
- What if *Olympic* had NOT dropped a propeller blade in March, delaying *Titanic*'s voyage to April?
- What if *Olympic* had been unable to deliver extra coal to fuel *Titanic* on her maiden voyage?
- What if Captain Haddock had served as *Titanic*'s captain on the maiden voyage?
- What if *Olympic* had left New York on time instead of two hours late?
- What if *Olympic* had been sailing at full steam instead of 18 knots to conserve coal?
- What if *Olympic* had reached *Titanic* in time?

Everyone involved in these events were changed by the experiences as they went back out into the world. Here's a look at what happened to some of the key participants in the years that followed the *Titanic* disaster.

CAPTAIN HADDOCK

Herbert J. Haddock continued to serve as *Olympic*'s captain after her 1913 refit. He and his ship finally got a chance to be of assistance to a sinking ship when the battleship HMS *Audacious* struck a mine on the morning of October 27 1914, just off the Irish coast. The *Olympic* raced to the sinking warship's side from 10 miles away and immediately launched fourteen lifeboats to rescue the *Audacious* crew. Despite attempts by Haddock to tow the sinking ship, the sea claimed *Audacious* the same night. The Admiralty later praised Haddock and his crew for their efforts. At the outset of the First World War, *Olympic* was laid up alongside other large liners, and the Admiralty put Haddock in command of a fleet of dummy battleships stationed in Belfast. Haddock never again commanded *Olympic*. Haddock died at age eighty-five on October 4, 1946.[1]

EDWARD DANIEL ALEXANDER 'ALEC' BAGOT

Olympic's junior wireless operator returned to his homeland in South Australia prior to the onset of the First World War. He served in the 1st Australian Wireless Signal Squadron in Mesopotamia, where he later founded a trading company. Returning to Australia again in 1925, he tried a number of business ventures before helping to found a political organization called the Citizens' League of South Australia. His political activism led him to the South Australian Legislative Council, on which he served in 1938–41. He returned to the insurance business in 1944. Upon his retirement in 1963 he wrote a biography called *Coppin the Great, Father of the Australian Theatre*. Bagot died of leukemia at age seventy-four in June 1968.[2]

ELLA WHEELER WILCOX

Soon after she reached England on board *Olympic*, writer Ella Wheeler Wilcox learned of Morgan Robertson's haunting story *Futility*, which was written more than ten years before the *Titanic* disaster but predicted the calamity with surreal accuracy. Wilcox was fascinated by Robertson's tale, which 'had given a picture of the *Olympic* and *Titanic* which was almost photographic in detail', and had called his ship the *Titan*.[3]

She wrote to the author to learn more about his novel and got the following explanation from Robertson:

As to the motif of my story, I merely tried to write a good story with no idea of being a prophet. But, as in other stories of mine, and in the work of other and better writers, coming discoveries and events have been anticipated. I do not doubt that it is because all creative writers get into a hypnoid, telepathic and percipient condition, in which, while apparently awake, they are half asleep, and tap, not only the better informed minds of others but the subliminal realm of unknown facts. Some, as you know, believe that in this realm there is no such thing as Time, and the fact that a long dream can occur in an instant of time gives color to it, and partly explains prophecy.

Robertson's reply failed to satisfy Ella, who wondered,

In the realm of unknown facts, was it already recorded fourteen years previously that the *Titanic* should sink? And how should Mr Robertson fix on almost the very name which was afterward given to the ill-fated sea monster?

Ella's husband, Robert, died in 1916. His loss sent her into a deep depression that turned her interest in mysticism and the occult into an obsession. A prolific poet, she is perhaps best known for 'Solitude,' which contained the lines 'Laugh, and the world laughs with you; Weep, and you weep alone'. She completed her autobiography, *The Worlds and I*, in 1918. She died of cancer at age sixty-eight on October 30, 1919.

MADAME SIMONE

Moved by her experience on the *Olympic* and eager to assist with the *Titanic* relief efforts for survivors and victims' families, Madame Simone returned to America in order to perform at the Women's *Titanic* Memorial benefit performance at the Century Theater on Friday, December 6, 1912.

The performance started as a light-hearted entertainment. It wasn't until after Madame Simone recited her poem – 'in perfect Parisian,' according to one writer – that Francis Wilson made the first reference of the evening to the *Titanic* disaster when he said:

We are here to help rear a monument to the nobility of American manhood and American womanhood. When our children look on that monument they will say, "Thank God I belong to that race which in the hour of sorest trial said 'Ladies first.'"[4]

Mrs John Hays Hammond, executive committee chairwoman for the event, later remarked:

This is the first time in the history of our material country, that a monument will have been erected to an ideal. It is surely as splendid a thing to help lift the standards of a people in this way to put up hospitals. A great many sculptors have offered to submit designs for the memorial in the competition which will be held.[5]

Seats for the benefit cost between 50 cents and $5 apiece, although First Lady Helen Taft watched from a special box that cost $1,000.

Tragedy again befell Madame Simone during the First World War. Her husband, Claude Casimir-Perier, joined the 108th Infantry Regiment as a lieutenant. He was reported missing on January 29, 1915. His wife and family were told that he'd been severely wounded and taken prisoner. They hoped for his safe return, hopes that were cruelly dashed on April 1, 1915, when it was confirmed that he had in fact been killed in battle and buried near Rheims, 80 miles north-east of Paris.[6]

Madame Simone was featured in an article called 'Widowed by the War,' which said:

At first society, which is more conservative in France than in England, was shocked at the marriage, but the two lived very happy together and Casimir-Perier had won a distinguished public position before his death.[7]

R. H. BENSON

Robert Hugh Benson had stirred the Anglican establishment in England with his conversion to the Catholic faith. By 1914 he was a monsignor. He wrote fifteen novels that explored the intricacies of faith and doubt. His historical novel *Come Rack, Come Rope!* recounted the horrors of the Reformation, when priests in England were tortured and killed. Benson often wrote of death, and a combination of heart trouble and exhaustion brought him to his own untimely end at age forty-two on October 19, 1914.[8]

MORTIMER SCHIFF

The Schiffs' legal case against their former valet, which they had sought to forget with the European vacation they sought on board *Olympic*, continued to haunt them after the *Titanic* disaster. Upon their return to America, their former valet was back in court in an attempt to secure his release from prison. The effort was eventually successful, and in early 1913, Foulke E. Brandt travelled to Minnesota to 'forget the past.'[9] Schiff continued to work at the financial firm of Kuhn, Loeb & Co. until his death, but his passion was the development of scouting in the United States. He began a long term as vice president of Boy Scouts of America in 1910 and was featured on the cover of *Time* magazine on February 14, 1927. One month after being elected president of the organization, he died on June 4, 1931, one day shy of his fifty-fourth birthday.[10]

DANIEL BURNHAM

Chicago's famed architect Daniel Burnham knew he was dying when he boarded *Olympic*, but he could never have imagined he'd lose his friend and colleague Frank Millet during the voyage. As he wrote to Millet's widow, 'I am not to live long without him,' and, characteristically, he was right. Burnham died just weeks after the sinking, on June 1, 1912, while enjoying his last European vacation with his wife, Margaret.

In a tribute to the late architect, President Taft said:

The news of Mr Burnham's death greatly shocks me. Mr Burnham was one of the foremost architects of the world, but he had more than mere professional skill. He had breadth of view as to artistic subjects that permitted him to lead in every movement for the education of the public in art or the development of art in every branch of our busy life. Without pay, at my insistence, he visited the Philippine Islands in order to make plans for the beautification of Manila and for the laying out of a capital in the mountains in the fine climate of Bagulo.

He was at the head of the Fine Arts commission, and I venture to say that there was no man in the professional life of the United States who has given more of his life to the public, without having filled public office, than Daniel Burnham. His death is a real loss to the whole community.[11]

FRANCIS MILLET

Burnham's great friend Francis Millet, sixty-five, died on the *Titanic*. Millet never reached New York to receive the letter Burnham had left him regarding the selection of a designer for the Lincoln Memorial. The work continued, however, and as Burnham had hoped, the job went to Henry Bacon, and work began on the memorial in February 1914.

Millet's body was the 249th to be recovered from the sea by the *Mackay Bennet*. Like all victims identified as coming from First Class, Millet's body was embalmed, placed in a casket and returned to shore. He was buried at East Bridgewater Central Cemetery in Boston.[12]

MAJOR ARCHIBALD BUTT

Major Archibald Butt, forty-five, died on the *Titanic*. When President Taft learned of the disaster, he dispatched the USS *Chester* in search of answers about the fate of his friend and military aide. When confirmation of Butt's death arrived, Taft issued a statement in tribute to his lost aide:

Major Archie Butt was my military aid. He was like a member of my family, and I feel his loss as if he had been a younger brother. The chief trait of his character was loyalty to his ideals, his cloth, and his friends. His character was a simple one, in the sense that he was incapable of intrigue or insincerity.

He was gentle and considerate to every one, high and low. He never lost, under any conditions, his sense of proper regard to what he considered the respect due to constituted authority. He was an earnest member of the Episcopal Church and loved that communion. He was a soldier, every inch of him; a most competent and successful Quartermaster and a devotee of his profession.

After I heard that part of the ship's company had gone down I gave up hope for the rescue of Major Butt, unless by accident. I knew that he would certainly remain on the ship's deck until every duty had been performed and every sacrifice made that properly fell on one charged, as he would feel himself charged, with responsibility for the rescue of others.

He leaves the widest circle of friends, whose memory of him is sweet in every particular.

Major Butt's body was never recovered. A memorial service was conducted on May 5 in Washington, DC, where a fountain was later erected in memory of Butt and Millet.[13]

JOSEPH BRUCE ISMAY

Bruce Ismay spent the rest of his life in the shadow of the *Titanic* disaster, never fully overcoming the stigma associated with the disaster and his role in it. Press coverage of his comportment was blistering, and he was labeled a coward for surviving when more than 1,500 others had died aboard his ship. Ismay resigned as president of International Mercantile Marine and chairman of the White Star Line in June 1913. He spent the rest of his life in seclusion, making his principal residence a cottage in County Galway, Ireland. Ismay was diagnosed with diabetes in the 1930s and eventually lost part of his right leg due to complications of the disease. He managed to outlive the White Star Line and the *Olympic*; he died at age seventy-four on October 17, 1937 in London.[14]

PHILIP FRANKLIN

IMM Vice President at the time of the *Titanic* disaster, Philip Franklin became a prime witness at the US Senate inquiry into the sinking. His testimony was spread over several days. Addressing confusion as to when he knew the truth about the *Titanic*, Franklin maintained that 'our first really authentic information came from Capt. Haddock.' When Ismay resigned as IMM president in 1913, the job went to Franklin, who managed to save the company from bankruptcy in part due to the wartime demand for ships. When Lord Pirrie died in 1924, Franklin was part of the entourage that escorted the body on board the *Olympic* for the voyage home. Shortly thereafter, IMM shareholders voted to sell the troubled White Star Line back to British interests. The transfer took place in 1927.[15]

J. P. MORGAN

The American financier whose shipping conglomerate, International Merchantile Marine, had made the *Olympic* and *Titanic* possible, didn't make the maiden voyage of the *Titanic* and wouldn't live to see the first anniversary of her sinking. News of the tragedy reached him while he was on his usual summer holiday in Europe – and he was said to be deeply affected by the disaster. His last birthday came just two days later, but he certainly wasn't in any mood to celebrate. He cancelled a ceremony planned for April 19 to dedicate a sanitarium in honor of his former physician and continued to wire friends in New York for news of the *Titanic* and her passengers and crew. The reclusive tycoon's health declined in the coming months. He made his European trip again the following spring, but he fell ill in March 1913 during a stay in Rome. Doctors 'could not induce the patient to eat because of the lack of functional vitality in the nerve centers. The refusal of throat muscles to do their duty made it impossible for Morgan to swallow.'[16] Ironically, plans were made to transport him by special train, but just as with the case of the *Titanic* special train to Halifax the year before, this proved unfounded. His condition worsened and he died at age seventy-five on March 31, 1913 at Rome's Grand Hotel. His body was returned to the United States aboard the French Line's *France*.[17]

LORD PIRRIE

Lord Pirrie mourned the loss of his nephew, Thomas Andrews, and made sure his shipyard learned from the unthinkable loss of the *Titanic*. Lessons learned from the disaster were used to refit *Olympic* and alter plans for *Gigantic*, later launched as *Britannic*. He remained active in shipping throughout the war and for the rest of his life. He was elected to the Northern Ireland Senate in 1921.

Pirrie died at age seventy-seven of pneumonia while en route to a business meeting in South America on board the Pacific Steam Navigation Company's liner *Ebro*. Philip Franklin broke the news to the world, declaring:[18]

> The death of Lord Pirrie will be a great blow to the shipping world and to his large circle of friends in all quarters of the globe. He was a remarkably active man for his years.
> Lord Pirrie was a progressive shipbuilder and always on the lookout for new ideas. When the adoption of oil fuel for steamships instead of coal became general in the shipping industry he was not satisfied to take the reports of experts as to the

production of petroleum in the Mexican oil fields, but made a special trip to Mexico to see for himself what the conditions were and how long the supply would probably last. Lord Pirrie always looked ahead and always was ready to hear any one who had any new ideas that might be of use in the shipbuilding industry.

The late J. P. Morgan was the promoter of the so-called Morgan combine and Lord Pirrie was the most influential factor in bringing the shipping companies together so that the corporation now known as the International Mercantile Marine Company could be organized with success.

Pirrie as the head of Harland & Wolff's shipyard at Belfast had built the modern steamships for the White Star, Red Star, Atlantic Transport, Dominion and Leyland Lines and had large holdings in these companies which enabled him to influence their sale to the late J. P. Morgan's newly created combine of Atlantic steamship lines.

Ebro returned Lord Pirrie's body to New York, where a White Star crew was waiting to carry the coffin aboard the *Olympic*, Pirrie's favorite ship, for the voyage home to England. Philip Franklin escorted the widow on board as the coffin was carried to an E-deck stateroom that had been draped in black and purple for the sad occasion.[19]

Pirrie was buried in Belfast City Cemetery. His marker includes a special etching that depicts the RMS *Olympic*.

CAPTAIN ROSTRON AND THE *CARPATHIA*

Captain Rostron won the admiration of the world for his ship's role in rescuing the survivors of the *Titanic*. He testified before both the American and British inquiries into the disaster. On a subsequent arrival to New York harbor, he was greeted by survivor Margaret Brown, who presented him with a loving cup on behalf of her fellow survivors. Congress also struck a special medal in his honor. He was in command of the *Carpathia* for another year before he transferred to the *Caronia* and later the *Carmania*, *Campania* and *Lusitania*. He served as a troop ship commander during the First World War. *Carpathia* was among the British steamers enlisted for service as a troop ship. She was torpedoed and sunk by a German U-boat on July 17, 1918 while steaming as part of a convoy off the coast of Ireland.[20] After the war, Rostron assumed command of *Mauretania* when she returned to passenger service in 1919. He was named commodore of the Cunard fleet in 1928 and retired in 1931. Rostron died at age seventy-one of pneumonia on November 4, 1940 and was buried in Southampton.

CAPTAIN STANLEY LORD AND THE *CALIFORNIAN*

While neither investigation into the *Titanic* disaster laid any specific charges at the feet of Captain Lord, his reputation, like that of Bruce Ismay, was damaged beyond repair as the captain of a ship that was near enough to see *Titanic*'s rockets yet failed to act. Captain Lord left the Leyland Line in August 1912. The following year, he joined the

Nitrate Producers Steamship Company. *Californian* was enlisted as a troop ship in the First World War and was torpedoed and sunk by a German U-boat on Nov. 9, 1915 off the Greek coast. Lord retired in 1928. When *A Night to Remember* was made into a film, Lord took offense at the way he was portrayed and sought to clear his name with help from the Mercantile Marine Service Association. His petition was denied. Lord died of kidney disease at age eighty-four on January 24, 1962.

LUSITANIA AND *MAURETANIA*

The Cunard ships whose emergence on the scene inspired the *Olympic* and *Titanic* were to suffer similar fates. Just three years after the *Titanic* disaster, *Lusitania* also sank as the victim of a German U-boat's torpedo on May 7, 1915 off the Irish coast. The sinking, which claimed the lives of 1,198 people, shocked the world and helped to draw the United States, which lost 128 citizens in the disaster, into the First World War. *Mauretania*, like *Olympic*, enjoyed a long and celebrated career. *Mauretania* captured the coveted Blue Riband for her speed in her first year of service and held it for twenty-two years. After the war she was updated and returned to passenger service. By 1934, when Cunard and White Star merged, she was withdrawn from service. In July 1935, she was sailed to Rosyth on the coast of Scotland for scrapping.

THE *BRITANNIC* (FORMERLY THE *GIGANTIC*)

Construction on the third *Olympic* class vessel was halted when her sister *Titanic* was lost. After the official inquiries were concluded, the ship was given a new name, *Britannic*, and a new plan that incorporated lessons learned from flaws in the *Titanic*'s design. The ship was given a double hull, and six of her fifteen watertight bulkheads were extended as high as B Deck. The ship was also given a new type of lifeboat davit that resembled a large crane and was capable of launching six lifeboats apiece. *Britannic* was launched on February 26, 1914. By August, as *Britannic* was being fitted out, Britain had entered the First World War. The new ship was enlisted into service as soon as possible. She was being prepared for war when *Lusitania* was sunk by a U-boat in May 1915. With many of her luxurious fittings resting in storage ashore, *Britannic* entered service as a hospital ship on December 23, 1915. While her sister *Olympic* served as a troop ship, *Britannic* became His Majesty's Hospital Ship *Britannic* with her immense hull painted white with a green stripe running horizontally along her sides and large red crosses attached amidships. She had made five successful trips to and from the war front, carrying the injured back to Britain. On her sixth mission, she was struck by a mine or torpedo on the morning of November 21, 1916 off the Kea Channel near Greece. Fifty-five minutes later, the ship sank with a loss of thirty lives. It was another terrible loss for the White Star Line. *Britannic* never carried a fare-paying passenger but had instead gained the distinction of being the biggest ship to fall victim to the war.

RMS *TITANIC*

Titanic was meant to be the middle of three ocean-going steamers that would ferry the rich (and, more lucratively, the immigrants) to and from America via the North Atlantic. But in one terrible moment, she found herself the victim of a collision that would make her name synonymous with disaster. She had been due to arrive in New York on April 17 but instead sank within three hours of the collision, taking 1,500 lives with her. Some of the wealthier families involved in the tragedy considered plans to drop dynamite on the wreck site in an effort to bring their loved ones' bodies to the surface, but such plans were dropped when the bodies of John Jacob Astor and other notable victims were later recovered from the sea by ships searching the wreck site. *Titanic's* grave remained unvisited for seventy-three years until a US–French expedition discovered the wreck site in September 1985. She rests more than two and a half miles down at 41°43'55"N 49°56'45"W. The ship lies in two large pieces. The bow is largely intact but the stern is a confusing tangle of steel and debris. Between the bow and stern lies an enormous field of debris that includes shoes, luggage, safes and shipboard supplies such as dinnerware and wine bottles. More than 6,000 objects have been recovered from the wreck site and put on display in exhibits that continue to travel the globe. Scientists now predict that within the next fifty years – perhaps sooner – *Titanic*, once the pride of the White Star Line, will be a rust stain on the bottom of the Atlantic.

RMS *OLYMPIC*

Once thought to be the unlucky sister for mishaps in the first year of her sea-faring career, *Olympic* would be the only ship among her two sisters to complete a regular-service voyage. After the events of April 14–15, 1912 she was often referred to as the sister ship to the *Titanic* – but hers was a long, distinguished career. When her country entered the First World War, *Olympic* was pressed into service as a troop ship. From September 1915 through 1918, *Olympic* carried more troops than any of the other big liners in war service, earning herself the nickname 'Old Reliable.' She earned another distinction as the only merchant ship to sink an enemy submarine during the war when, on May 12, 1918, she rammed and sank the German submarine U-103. At war's end *Olympic* underwent another refit that made her the first large liner to make the conversion from coal to oil-burning boilers. In 1920 she returned to passenger service, and by 1929 was enjoying the biggest passenger lists in years. *Olympic* had recently undergone yet another refit when two events of 1934 helped to spell the end. On May 15, *Olympic* collided with the Nantucket Lightship in a dense fog on May 15. Four men on board the lightship were killed. That same year, Cunard merged with the White Star Line and began evaluating the future of the fleet. *Olympic* and *Mauretania* were both retired from service. For a time there was talk of her becoming a floating hotel, but she was sold to Sir John Jarvis for £100,000. Her inner furnishings were sold at auction, and she departed Southampton for the last time on October 11, 1935 bound for Jarrow in northern England, where she would be partially demolished. In 1937, what remained was towed to Inverkeithing in Scotland for final demolition. By early 1939, she was gone.

Notes

CHAPTER 1: 'MESSAGE RECEIVED: IT'S SOS'

1 'Two British Lords to Farm in Canada', *The New York Times*, April 11, 1912, p. 1.
2 'Sailing of *Olympic* Starts Rush Abroad', *The New York Times*, April 14, 1912, p. 1.
3 'Chorus Girls Best of Wives For Rich Men', *The Logansport Pharos* (Logansport, Indiana), March 20, 1912, p. 6.
4 *The Hull Index* (Sioux City, Iowa), March 9, 1912, p. 2.
5 'America and France Least Hypocritical of Nations', *The New York Times*, October 27, 1912, p. SM4.
6 'Sees Canal Boom Menacing America', *The New York Times*, April 14, 1912, p. C-1.
7 'Mme. Simone's Marriage', *The New York Times*, November 20, 1909.
8 'Got Tragic News at Sea', *The New York Times*, May 12, 1912.
9 'Grand Jury Acquits Schiff and Attorney', *The Constitution* (Atlanta, GA), March 29, 1912, p. 1B.
10 'Englishmen Dig for Temple of King Solomon', *San Antonio Light and Gazette*, December 19, 1909.
11 *The Evening Tribune* (Marysville, Ohio), April 6, 1912, p. 1.
12 *The Letters of Arturo Toscanini*, edited by Harvey Sachs, 2002, Alfred A. Knopf, p. 85.
13 Testimony, Ernest Moore, United States Senate Inquiry, *Titanic* disaster, Day 18 (May 25, 1912), and submitted process verbal (wireless log).
14 'World Famous Architect Dead', *Free Press* (Winnipeg), June 8, 1912, p. 1.
15 *Daniel H. Burnham: Architect, Planner of Cities*, by Charles Moore, 1921, Houghton Mifflin Company, pp. 154–5.
16 *The Maiden Voyage*, by Geoffrey Marcus, 1969, The Viking Press, p. 195.
17 Margaret Burnham's Daybook, Daniel H. Burnham Collection, Ryerson and Burnham Archives, The Art Institute of Chicago.
18 *Daniel H. Burnham: Architect, Planner of Cities*, by Charles Moore, 1921, Houghton Mifflin Company, pp. 154–5.

CHAPTER 2: 'WHAT IS THE MATTER WITH YOU?'

1   *A Night to Remember*, by Walter Lord, 1955, Henry Holt and Company, p. 16.

2   *A Night to Remember*, by Walter Lord, 1955, Henry Holt and Company, p. 70.

3   *The Truth about the Titanic*, by Col. Archibald Gracie, reprinted 1985, Sutton Publishing Limited, pp. 128–129.

4   *Nellie Taft: The Unconventional First Lady of the Ragtime Era*, by Carl Sferrazza Anthony, 2005, HarperCollins Publishers Inc., pp. 332–335.

5   'Lusitania Finished', *The Daily Gleaner* (Kingston, Jamaica), June 4, 1907, p. 1.

6   '*Cedric*: The Largest Possible Ship', *The Salt Lake Tribune*, April 5, 1903, p. 25.

7   '*Olympic* and *Titanic*', *The Daily Gleaner* (Kingston, Jamaica), Sept. 22, 1908.

8   'The Builders of the *Olympic* and *Titanic*', *Olympic and Titanic: Ocean Liners of the Past*, Patrick Stephens Limited (Third Edition; 1988), p. 7.

9   *Fairbanks Daily News-Miner* (Fairbanks, Alaska), Oct. 10, 1910, p. 1.

10   'She Will Make a Big Splash When She is Launched', *Middletown Times-Press* (Middletown, NY), Oct. 20, 1910, p. 6.

11   'Biggest Steamer Launched', *The Washington Post*, Oct. 21, 1910, p. 10.

12   *Titanic Voices: Memories from the Fateful Voyage*, by Donald Syslop, Alastair Forsyth, Sheila Jemima, 1997, Sutton Publishing Limited, p. 35.

13   *Titanic Voices: Memories from the Fateful Voyage*, by Donald Syslop, Alastair Forsyth, Sheila Jemima, 1997, Sutton Publishing Limited, p. 33.

14   *Titanic Voices: Memories from the Fateful Voyage*, by Donald Syslop, Alastair Forsyth, Sheila Jemima, 1997, Sutton Publishing Limited, p. 34.

15   *Titanic Survivor: The Newly Discovered Memoirs of Violet Jessop Who Survived Both the Titanic and Britannic Disasters*, by Violet Jessop (edited and annotated by John Maxtone-Graham), 1997, Sheridan House, Inc., p. 102.

CHAPTER 3: 'LIGHTING UP ALL POSSIBLE BOILERS'

1   Testimony, Ernest Moore, United States Senate Inquiry, *Titanic* disaster, Day 18 (May 25, 1912), and submitted process verbal (wireless log).

2   'The Largest Ship in the World', *The Gleaner* (Kingston, Illinois), Nov. 3, 1910.

3   'Biggest of All the Ocean Liners' *Marysville Tribune* (Marysville, Ohio), Dec. 29, 1909, p. 2

4   'Fifty Years of Gradual Neglect of Safety for Ships', *The New York Times*, Aug. 11, 1912.

5   'The Story of the *Titanic* as Told by Its Survivors', *The Loss of the SS Titanic*, by Lawrence Beesley, 1960, Reprinted by Dover Publications, Inc., 1960, p. 35.

6   *The Night Lives On*, by Walter Lord, 1986, William Morrow and Company, Inc., p. 116.

7   *A Night to Remember*, by Walter Lord, 1955, Henry Holt and Company, p. 89.

8   'The Story of the *Titanic* as Told by Its Survivors', *The Loss of the SS Titanic*, by Lawrence Beesley, 1960, reprinted by Dover Publications, Inc., 1960, p. 41.

9   *The Maiden Voyage*, by Geoffrey Marcus, 1969, The Viking Press, page 40.

CHAPTER 4: 'WELL KNOWN TO WHITE STAR TRAVELERS'

1 *Titanic Survivor: The Newly Discovered Memoirs of Violet Jessop Who Survived Both the Titanic and Britannic Disasters*, by Violet Jessop, 1997, Sheridan House, Inc., pp. 164-65.
2 *The World* (New York), April 25, 1896, p. 5.
3 *The New York Times*, April 21, 1899, p. 2.
4 *The New York Times*, Aug. 10, 1898.
5 *The Post-Standard* (Syracuse, NY), March 11, 1901, p. 2.
6 *The New York Times*, Aug. 8, 1902, p. 12.
7 The New York Times, Feb. 21, 1903.
8 'The Largest Ship Afloat', *The New York Times*, Feb. 8, 1903, p. 12.
9 'Biggest Steamer Afloat', *The Washington Post*, July 9, 1904, p. 11.
10 *The Salt Lake Tribune*, April 5, 1903, p. 25.
11 'Liner *Cedric* in Port', *The New York Times*, Feb. 21, 1903.
12 *The Weekly Gazette* (Colorado Springs, Colo.), March 12, 1903, p. 9.
13 '*Cedric* is Sunk', *The Logansport Journal* (Logansport, Indiana), Nov. 26, 1903.
14 'No Fear for the *Cedric*', *The New York Times*, Nov. 26, 1903, p. 6.
15 '"A Cruel Hoax," Say *Cedric*'s Owners', *The World* (New York), Nov. 26, 1903.
16 *The New York Times*, Nov. 28, 1903, p. 3.
17 *The New York Times*, March 21, 1905, p. 6
18 'Four Buried at Sea', *The New York Times*, June 30, 1906, p. 2.
19 *Titanic and Other Ships*, by Charles H. Lightoller, reprinted 2007, Historia Press, pp. 209-10.
20 'Largest Ship is Due to Arrive in New York', *The Ogden Standard* (Ogden City, Utah), May 16, 1907, p. 1.
21 'Liner *Oceanic* Afire at Her Pier', *The New York Times*, June 2, 1907, p. 1.
22 '2 Titled Smokers', *The Washington Post*, Jan. 26, 1908, p. 1.
23 '*Oceanic* Broke Propeller', *The New York Times*, Jan. 8, 1909, p. 16.
24 'King Decorates White Star Officers', *The New York Times*, Nov. 24, 1909, p. 6.
25 '*Oceanic* Sinks Coal Barge', *The Washington Post*, Nov. 24, 1910, p. 5.
26 'Lightning Strikes Liner *Oceanic*', *Naugatuck Daily News* (Naugatuck, Connecticut), March 23, 1911, p. 5.
27 'Get Giants of the Sea', *New-York Tribune*, Dec. 2, 1910.

CHAPTER 5: '*OLYMPIC* IS A MARVEL'

1 *The Daily Bulletin* (Brownwood, Texas), June 14, 1911, p. 5.
2 'Change in Commodores', *The New York Times*, June 6, 1911.
3 '*Olympic* Crew Win', *The New York Times*, June 11, 1911.
4 *Titanic Survivor: The Newly Discovered Memoirs of Violet Jessop Who Survived Both the Titanic and Britannic Disasters*, by Violet Jessop, 1997, Sheridan House, Inc., p. 102.

5   'The *Olympic* Sails', *The New York Times*, June 15, 1911, p. 1.

6   'The *Olympic* Like a City', *The New York Times*, June 18, 1911.

7   *Titanic Survivor: The Newly Discovered Memoirs of Violet Jessop Who Survived Both the Titanic and Britannic Disasters*, by Violet Jessop, 1997, Sheridan House, Inc., p. 104.

8   'Giant New Liner Ends First Trip', *Trenton Evening Times* (Trenton, New Jersey), June 22, 1911, p. 11.

9   *Titanic Survivor: The Newly Discovered Memoirs of Violet Jessop Who Survived Both the Titanic and Britannic Disasters*, by Violet Jessop, 1997, Sheridan House, Inc., p. 105.

10   'Aeroplane Above Outgoing *Olympic*', *The New York Times*, June 29, 1911.

11   'Dined on the *Olympic*', *The Altoona Mirror* (Altoona, PA), July 22, 1911, p. 5.

12   *The Des Moines News*, July 24, 1911, p. 3.

13   'New Vessel Will Be Built by White Star Line as Sister Ship of *Olympic*', *The Tipton Daily Tribune* (Tipton, Indiana), July 24, 1911, p. 3.

14   'Dinner to Capt. Smith of the *Olympic*', *The New York Times*, Aug. 17, 1911.

15   *The Racine Daily Journal* (Racine, WI), Aug. 31, 1911, p. 10.

16   'Runs to Kiss His Wife', *Evening Independent* (Massillon, Ohio), Sept. 11, 1911, p. 1.

17   'A Record Passenger List', *The New York Times*, Sept. 17, 1911.

18   'Crawled Through Porthole', *The New York Times*, Sept. 21, 1911.

19   'Recent Collision of the *Olympic*', *The Gleaner* (Kingston, Ill.), Oct. 6, 1911, p. 22.

20   'Recent Collision of the *Olympic*', The Gleaner (Kingston, Ill.), Oct. 6, 1911, p. 22.

21   'Rivals aid White Star', *The New York Times*, Sept. 23, 1911.

22   '*Olympic* Sails to Belfast', *The New York Times*, Oct. 5, 1911.

23   'The *Olympic* Sails for Port', *The New York Times*, Dec. 1, 1911.

24   '*Olympic* Back with a Budget of News', *The New York Times*, Dec. 8, 1911.

25   'Hustle on the *Olympic*', *The New York Times*, Dec. 9, 1911.

26   'Morgan in Paris', *The New York Times*, Jan. 6, 1912.

27   'Change Runs of Liners', *The New York Times*, Jan. 8, 1912.

28   'Big Seas Pound *Olympic*', *The Washington Post*, Jan. 18, 1912, p. 4.

29   'Astor Marriage is Denounced', *Logansport Daily Reporter*, Aug. 8, 1911, p. 5.

30   'Minister is Found to Tie Astor-Force Knot for Big Fee', *The Janesville Daily Gazette* (Janesville, Wisconsin), Sept. 7, 1911, p. 1.

31   'For Sale – Woman', *The Marshall Statesman* (Marshall, Michigan), Sept. 22, 1911, p. 14.

32   'Astor Dinner Off: New York '400' Would Know Reason', *Oakland Tribune* (Oakland, California), Jan. 13, 1912, p. 10.

33   'Guesses It First Time', *The Tipton Daily Tribune* (Tipton, Indiana), Jan. 26, 1912, p. 7.

34   '*Olympic* Strikes Submerged Wreck', *The New York Times*, Feb. 28, 1912.

35   'Dr. Pease Home from Long Jaunt', *The Evening Independent* (Massilon, Ohio), March 21, 1912, p. 1.

CHAPTER 6: 'WE'VE LOST TOUCH'

1   Testimony, Ernest Moore, United States Senate Inquiry, *Titanic* disaster, Day 18 (May 25, 1912), and submitted process verbal (wireless log).
2   *Great Shipwrecks of the 20th Century*, by Thomas E. Bonsall, 1988, Bookman Dan!, Inc., p. 35.
3   'How Binns Flashed His Calls for Help', *The New York Times*, Jan. 26, 1909.
4   *Trenton Evening News* (Trenton, N.J.), Jan. 26, 1909, p. 6.

CHAPTER 7: 'MORE SERIOUS NEWS MIGHT COME LATER'

1   'Staffer on Duty When *Titanic* Sank Tells How AP Covered 1912 Disaster', by Charles E. Crane, AP World, Spring 1959.
2   'Correspondence: J. Bruce Ismay and Philip Franklin – 1911', Papers of J Bruce Ismay, White Star Line, National Museums Liverpool, Maritime Archives and Library.
3   *A Night to Remember*, by Walter Lord, 1955, Henry Holt and Company, pp. 136-137.
4   *The Worlds and I*, by Ella Wheeler Wilcox, 1918, George H. Doran Company, p. 219.
5   'Why Was the Truth of *Titanic* Disaster Kept Back?', *The Daily Mirror*, April 22, 1912, p. 3.
6   *The Worlds and I*, by Ella Wheeler Wilcox, 1918, George H. Doran Company, p. 219.
7   'Got Tragic News at Sea', *The New York Times*, May 12, 1912.
8   '*Olympic* Reaches England', The Lima News (Lima, Ohio), April 20, 1912, front page.
9   'Captain of the *Titanic*'s Sister Ship Denies That He Sent Messages of Hope', *New York Herald*, April 21, 1912, p. 5.
10 *Titanic Voices: Memories from the Fateful Voyage*, by Donald Syslop, Alastair Forsyth, Sheila Jemima, 1997, Sutton Publishing Limited, p. 176: Dorothy Cross (Southampton City Heritage Collection).

CHAPTER 8: 'THE AWFUL TRUTH'

1   Testimony, Ernest Moore, United States Senate Inquiry, *Titanic* disaster, Day 18 (May 25, 1912), and submitted process verbal (wireless log).
2   'News of Sinking at Cape Race 2 p.m.', *The New York Times*, April 22, 1912.
3   *A Night to Remember*, by Walter Lord, 1955, Henry Holt and Company, p. 154.
4   'False Message Fully Explained', *The New York Times*, April 22, 1912.
5   'The Cedric's Parrot Mascot', The New York Times, May 4, 1903, p. 2.
6   *A Night to Remember*, by Walter Lord, 1955, Henry Holt and Company, p. 160.

CHAPTER 9: 'THE SHIP IS IN GLOOM'

1   'False Message Fully Explained', *The New York Times*, April 22, 1912.

2   'Why Was the Truth of *Titanic* Disaster Kept Back?', *The Daily Mirror*, April 22, 1912, p. 3.

3   Daniel H. Burnham: Architect, Planner of Cities, by Charles Moore, 1921, Houghton Mifflin Company, pp. 154-5.

4   *The Worlds and I*, by Ella Wheeler Wilcox, 1918, George H. Doran Company, p. 219.

5   *The Maiden Voyage*, by Geoffrey Marcus, 1969, The Viking Press, p. 198.

6   Margaret Burnham's Daybook, Daniel H. Burnham Collection, Ryerson and Burnham Archives, The Art Institute of Chicago.

7   *The Scotsman*, April 17, 1912.

8   *Daily Sketch*, Thursday, April 18.

9   *The Carpathia and the Titanic: Rescue at Sea*, by George M. Behe, Lulu Press, 2011.

10 *The Maiden Voyage*, by Geoffrey Marcus, 1969, The Viking Press, p. 71.

11 *Titanic Survivor: The Newly Discovered Memoirs of Violet Jessop Who Survived Both the Titanic and Britannic Disasters*, by Violet Jessop, 1997, Sheridan House, Inc., p. 129.

12 *Titanic Voices: Memories from the Fateful Voyage*, by Donald Syslop, Alastair Forsyth, Sheila Jemima, 1997, Sutton Publishing Limited, p. 70.

13 *Titanic: Destination Disaster – The Legends and the Reality*, by John P. Eaton and Charles A. Haas, 1996, W.W. Norton & Company, Inc. (Revised and Expanded Edition), p. 94.

14 *Titanic Voices: Memories from the Fateful Voyage*, by Donald Syslop, Alastair Forsyth, Sheila Jemima, 1997, Sutton Publishing Limited, p. 106.

15 *Titanic and Other Ships*, by Commander C.H. Lightoller, Historia Press 2007; originally published 1935, p. 218.

16 *Nottingham Daily Express*, April 22, 1912.

17 *Wall Street People*, by Charles D. Ellis and James R. Vertin, 2003, John Wiley and Sons, Inc.

18 'Learned Details of the *Titanic* Disaster Today', The Rock Hill Herald, April 20, 1912.

19 *Titanic: A Journey Through Time*, by John Eaton and Charles Haas, 1999, W. W. Norton & Company, p. 87.

20 'Reported Finding of Bodies', *The Washington Post*, April 18, 1912, p. 11.

21 '*Olympic* Passenger Heard From', *The New Brunswick Times*, April 18, 1912.

22 *The Worlds and I*, by Ella Wheeler Wilcox, 1918, George H. Doran Company, p. 220.

23 'Captain's Widow Stricken', *Fort Gibson New Era* (Fort Gibson, Oklahoma), April 25, 1912, p. 2.

24 *The New York Times*, April 19, 1912.

CHAPTER 10: 'SO SAD A LANDING'

1 'Learned Details of the *Titanic* Disaster Today', *The Rock Hill Herald*, April 20, 1912.

2 *The Worlds and I*, by Ella Wheeler Wilcox, 1918, George H. Doran Company, p. 220.

3 *Titanic's Last Secrets*, by Brad Matsen, 2008, Twelve, an imprint of Grand Central Publishing, Hachette Book Group, USA, p. 212.

4 'Captain of the *Titanic*'s Sister Ship Denies That He Sent Messages of Hope', *New York Herald*, April 21, 1912, p. 5.

5 'Recover Bodies', *Fort Gibson New Era* (Fort Gibson, OK), April 25, 1912, p. 2.

6 'Bodies Cover the Sea', *The Washington Post*, April 25, 1912, p. 1.

7 Sympathy Letter to Mrs Frank Millet, The Francis Davis Millet and Millet family papers, Archives of American Art, Smithsonian Institution.

8 'Rush to Make *Olympic* Safe', *The New York Times*, April 22, 1913.

9 'The *Olympic* Messages', *The Daily Mail*, April 22, 1912, p. 11.

10 *The Daily Review* (Decatur, Illinois), April 23, 1912, p. 1.

11 *The Evening Tribune* (Albert Lea, Minnesota), April 22, 1912, p. 1.

12 '*Gigantic* to be Biggest Liner', *Middletown Daily Times-Press* (Middletown, New York), Nov. 24, 1911, p. 5.

13 *Newport Daily News* (Newport, Rhode Island), May 31, 1912, p. 1.

CHAPTER 11: THE AFTERMATH

1 'Why the *Olympic* was Delayed', *Lloyd's Weekly News*, April 28, 1912, p. 5.

2 'Crew Arrested; *Olympic* is Held', *Lock Haven Express* (Lock Haven, PA), April 27, 1912, p. 7.

3 '*Titanic*'s Sister Ship Headed for Rocks', *Titanic Commutator*, 1988, Volume 12, Titanic Historical Society.

4 *The Truth about the Titanic*, first published 1913, reprinted 1985, Sutton Publishing Limited, p. 58.

5 *The Syracuse Herald* (Syracuse, NY), July 7, 1912.

6 'Large Outlay', *The Gleaner* (Kingston, Jamaica), Aug. 14, 1912, p. 7.

7 '*Olympic* Broke Port Propeller', *The Lethbride Daily Herald*, Sept. 16, 1912, p. 9.

8 *The Janesville Daily Gazette* (Janesville, Wisconsin), March 24, 1913, p. 1.

9 'Refitted Steamship *Olympic* Sets Sail for New York', *The Janesville Daily Gazette* (Janesville, Wisconsin), April 2, 1913, p. 13.

10 'Can't Sink *Olympic*', *Indiana Evening Gazette*, April 3, 1912, p. 2.

11 'Glenn Marston, Xi '03, Tells of Conversation with Captain Smith, of the *Titanic*', *The Shield*: official publication of the Theta Delta Chi Fraternity, Volume 28, by Theta Delta Chi, pp. 186-188.

12 '*Titanic*: Death of a Dream', A&E Home Video documentary, 1994.

http://www.imdb.com/company/co0056790/

http://www.imdb.com/company/co0056790/"E Television Networks

http://www.imdb.com/company/co0005015/" Communications

CHAPTER 12: EPILOGUE

1   Haddock died Oct. 4, 1946. Verified, Chris Bussell, grave visit.

2   'Bagot, Edward Daniel Alexander (1893–1968)', *Australian Dictionary of Biography*, Volume 7, Melbourne University Press, 1979, pp. 132-133.

3   The Worlds and I, by Ella Wheeler Wilcox, published 1918 by George H. Doran Company, p. 220.

4   'Women Raise $10,000 by *Titanic* Benefit', *The New York Times*, Dec. 7, 1912.

5   'Splendid Prospects for *Titanic* Benefit', *The New York Times*, Dec. 4, 1912.

6   'Claude Casimir-Perier killed', *The New York Times*, April 1, 1915.

7   'Widowed by The War', *The Salt Lake Tribune*, Sunday, May 2, 1915, Magazine section.

8   'R. H. Benson: Unsung Genius', by Joseph Pearce, Jan./Feb. 2001, *Lay Witness*.

9   'Brandt Wants to Forget', *Middleton Daily Times-Press* (Middletown, NY), Jan. 21, 1913, p. 3.

10 'Schiff Gave Freely to Social Service', *The New York Times*, June 5, 1931.

11 'D.H. Burnham Dead', *The Washington Post*, Sunday, June 2, 1912, p. 7.

12 'Mr. Francis Davis Millet', Encyclopedia-Titanica.org. http://www.encyclopedia-titanica.org/titanic-biography/francis-davis-millet.html

13 'Taft Feels Loss of Aide as if He Had Been Brother', *Washington Times*, April 19, 1912.

14 *The New York Times*, Oct. 19, 1937.

15 'The White Star Line and the International Mercantile Marine Company', by William B Saphire, Titanic Historical Society.

16 'J.P. Morgan is Dead in Rome', *The Fort Wayne Daily News*, March 31, 1913, p. 2.

17 'J. Pierpont Morgan, Great Financier, Dies in Rome', *New Brunswick Times* (New Brunswick, N.J.), March 31, 1913, p. 1, 3.

18 'Lord Pirrie Dies on Ship Bound Here', *The New York Times*, June 9, 1924, p. 1.

19 '*Olympic* Carries Pirrie's Body Home', *The New York Times*, June 14, 1924, p. 1.

20 '*Carpathia* Sunk; Five of Crew Killed', *The New York Times*, July 20, 1918, p. 4.

ACKNOWLEDGEMENTS:

This book would not have been possible without the care, attention and interest of Campbell McCutcheon, who saw the potential in this story and also gave generously of his photo collection so that it could come to life, and Louis Archard, who saw the manuscript through the editing and production process.

The author wishes to thank Ed and Karen Kamuda for their tireless efforts to keep the *Titanic* story alive through the auspices of the Titanic Historical Society.

Thanks also to Chris Bussell, who had been researching Captain Haddock ever since discovering he was living in the captain's former Southampton home. Sadly, Chris died before his project was complete. I remain saddened by his loss and grateful for his assistance.

My thanks also to George Behe for his generosity and graciousness in offering advice and sharing research sources, and to Charles Haas, President of the Titanic International Society, for his support and guidance.

Special thanks are also due to my friends Angie Scharnhorst and Nora Donaghy who graciously volunteered to proofread the manuscript.

Lastly, my thanks to my late aunt, Joann Mellies, without whose encouragement and interest through my years of studying the *Titanic*, this book would not have been possible. And to my extended family and friends for thing never-ending support. Special thanks are also due to my grandparents, Joy and Darrell Howard, who helped me put together the first public display of my *Titanic* memorabilia in the public library in our hometown of Overbrook, Kansas.

Index

ALSO AVAILABLE FROM AMBERLEY PUBLISHING

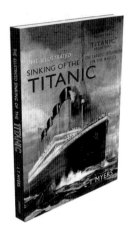

THE ILLUSTRATED SINKING OF THE TITANIC

In April 1912 the *Titanic* sank, taking 1,500 people to their deaths in the freezing Atlantic. Illustrated with many rare images, the book tells the story of the *Titanic*'s last few days, from accounts of the survivors on board RMS *Carpathia*. Published barely weeks after the ship sank, *The Sinking of the Titanic* has become a classic of disaster literature.

978-1-84868-053-1
192pp

THE ILLUSTRATED TRUTH ABOUT THE TITANIC

When the *Titanic* sank, Archibald Gracie was one of the last to escape, surviving because he crawled into the last lifeboat, which had floated off the ship upside down as it sank. Telling the story of *Titanic*'s final days, he was meticulous in his commentary of the sinking and his book, completed just before he died in 1913, is the definitive record of the doomed liner's last few hours.

978-1-84868-093-7
192pp

www.amberleybooks.com